You &
The Police!

by

Boston T. Party

Published by

*To Dewey ~
Stay FREE!
Boston XI/05*

JAVELIN PRESS

c/o P.O. Box 31Y, Ignacio, Colorado. (81137-0031)
(Without any 4 USC §§ 105-110 *"Federal area"* or *"State."*)
www.javelinpress.com

DISCLAIMER

First Printing: *February, 2005*
Printed in the united states of America,
without any 4 §§ 105-110 *"Federal area"* or *"State."*

15 14 13 12 11 10 9 8 7 6 5 4 3 2 1

2012 2011 2010 2009 2008 2007 2006 2005

ISBN 1-888766-09-3
www.javelinpress.com

ACKNOWLEDGMENTS

Great thanks go to my fabulous cover illustrator, the late Carrol O. Murphy. We miss you, Cowboy Artist.

I'm also hugely indebted to "Mr. T" for his third fantastic cover layout (after *Boston's Gun Bible* and *Molôn Labé!*). *"What—*I dunno mah *bidness?"*

I thank all my readers who have supported all books and wrote me such nice letters and emails.

For years I've admired the principles and courage of that lone voice of congressional reason, Dr. Ron Paul (R-TX). (They don't call him "Dr. No" for nothing.) He has been the champion of Liberty and the bane of Tyranny in the U.S. House for several terms, and was an outspoken critic of the so-called *USA PATRIOT Act* of 2001.

Special thanks to an undeserved blessing of a lady, to whom I am infinitely indebted for her joy, humor, patient support and unsinkable spirit—my mother.

DEDICATION

You & The Police! is dedicated to the lonely, courageous, and endangered **Peace Officer**—whose battleground is sadly also within the ranks, as well as on the streets. God bless and protect you all.

Works by Boston T. Party:

Good-Bye April 15th!

The untaxation classic—crystal clear and sweeping. Copied, plagiarized, and borrowed from, but never equaled. The most effective and least hazardous untaxation guide. Proven over 12 years and thousands of readers!

    392 pp. softcover (1992) $40 + $6 s&h (cash, please)

You & The Police!   (revised for 2005)

The definitive guide to your rights and tactics during police confrontations. When can you *refuse* to answer questions or consent to searches? Don't lose your liberty through ignorance! This 2005 edition covers the *USA PATRIOT Act* and much more.

    168 pp. softcover (2005) $16 + $5 s&h (cash, please)

Bulletproof Privacy

How to Live Hidden, Happy, and Free!

Explains precisely how to lay low and be left alone by the snoops, government agents and bureaucrats. Boston shares many of his own unique methods. The bestselling privacy book in America!

    160 pp. softcover (1997) $16 + $5 s&h (cash, please)

Hologram of Liberty

The Constitution's Shocking Alliance
with Big Government   by Kenneth W. Royce

The Convention of 1787 was the most brilliant and subtle *coup d'état* in history. The nationalist framers *designed* a strong government, guaranteed through purposely ambiguous verbiage. Many readers say this is Boston's best book. A jaw-dropper.

    262 pp. softcover (1997) $20 + $5 s&h (cash, please)

Boston on Surviving Y2K

And Other Lovely Disasters

Even though Y2K was Y2¿Qué? this title remains highly useful for all preparedness planning. **Now on sale for 50% off!** (It's the same book as The Military Book Club 's *Surviving Doomsday*.)

    352 pp. softcover (1998) only $11 + $5 s&h (in cash)

Boston's Gun Bible (new text for 2004)

A rousing how-to/*why*-to on modern gun ownership. Firearms are *"liberty's teeth"* and it's time we remembered it. Fully revised in 2002 with 10 new chapters. **200+ new pages were added!** Much more complete than the 2000 edition. No other general gun book is more thorough or useful! Indispensable!

    848 pp. softcover (2002) $28 + $6 s&h (cash, please)

Molôn Labé!   (Boston's first novel)

If you liked *Unintended Consequences* by John Ross and Ayn Rand's *Atlas Shrugged*, then Boston's novel will be a favorite. It dramatically outlines an innovative recipe for Liberty which could actually work! A thinking book for people of action; an action book for people of thought. A freedom classic!

    454 pp. softcover (2004) $24 + $6 s&h (cash, please)
    limited edition hardcover $44 + $6 (while supplies last)

www.javelinpress.com
www.freestatewyoming.org

TABLE OF CONTENTS

16   You & Your Guns

17   Our Dwindling Rights

PREFACE

Let me start off by saying that *You & The Police!* is not an exhaustive legal handbook. It could not be at a mere 168 pages. It is, however, a very comprehensive *guide* to the case law regarding your constitutional rights vs. the powers of the police. After absorbing this book, you'll know at least as much as the cops. Such is a probably good enough for most of us.

Even still, no one book could possibly be exhaustive as case law (unless/until it reaches the US Supreme Court) differs amongst the 94 US Districts, the 12 Appellate Circuits, and the 50 states themselves. While I can get you there 95% of the way, you'll have to do some local research to discover the finer points within your area (including your police department's policy on such things as vehicle inventories, telephonic warrants, etc.).

So, *please* don't write me that I painted issues with too broad a brush. A broad brush is the best I could do in 168 pages. If you want to learn more, simply visit www.findlaw.com. Learn how to use the West Publishing indices and how to "Shepardize" court cases. These legal issues are generally *not* terribly complex, even when interwoven, for the courts must distill their rulings to be digestible by the average cop.

Even if I *could* offer an exhaustive volume, such would become, paragraph by paragraph, slowly outdated. The law is not static, but dynamic. Though much of the case law regarding arrest, search and seizure, etc. is well established, there will always be at least *some* gradual encroachment on Liberty.

And, there is the ugly possibility of a pseudo-martial law wherein our rights are "temporarily" suspended. (I discuss this fully in the last chapter, *Our Dwindling Rights.*) If *that* occurs, then all bets are off and this book will be a bitter reminder of comparatively halcyon days.

So, case law is constantly making inroads on our rights, which could be swept away entirely if another *"PATRIOT Act"* passes. My point being: we *don't* have a lot of time left to assert and enjoy our residual rights. At "best" they're being slowly eroded. At worst, they will be nullified by Congressional fiat.

I cannot accept the notion that a police state is the price we must pay to live in a free country.

It's foolish whining to politicians while allowing the police to bluff and bully you. In the immediate sense, this is not a political battle. Politics follow, politics react, but politics do *not* initiate. We must win this war *individually* in real life, on the home-front of our streets and cities. Learn to assert and enjoy Liberty—while we may.

Wise up and toughen up. Get *angry*. America is fast turning into East Germany—*"Your papers!"* Get righteously indignant. We are losing our country, and not just at the macro level of national/international sellouts. We are losing America because we've grown afraid of government down to even the local level. Law abiding people are *afraid* of their police. That is *sick*. Let's get over this national wimpiness and ignorance.

This book isn't about "taking the law into our own hands." We *are* the law! We merely *delegate* it to the police and courts on condition of good stewardship. **Remember, the *purpose* of law is to facilitate a *reasonable* society.** The law is a *means*—not an end. The law is to serve *us*—we are not to serve the law. Let's all learn once again to be the *master*.

Boston T. Party
January 2005

Note: Also, if I mention something without fully covering it, be patient; I'll get to it a bit further on, or in a later chapter.

Case citations are easy to decipher. For example, take:

Berkemer v. McCarty, 468 U.S. 420, 439 (1984)

Berkemer is the petitioner; McCarty is the defendant.
468 is the Volume # of Supreme Court reporting service.
420 is the beginning page #, and 439 is page of quotation.

For research visit www.findlaw.com/casecode/supreme.html

❖ 1
YOU & THE LAW

We notice, with no pleasure, an increasing tendency toward what may be called javertism in our regulators. You remember Inspector Javert, the protagonist's nemesis in "Les Miserables" — "The law's the law, Jean Valjean. Good, bad, or indifferent, the law's the law!"

*Now then, this attitude may be fitting for a devout Jew, who holds that the law comes straight from God, and thus is not to be interpreted nor reasoned with in any way. However, to those of us who inherit the Anglo-Saxon tradition that the law is a temporal arrangement between the king and the people, which can and does change with circumstances, the law should be applied in an essentially <u>reasonable</u> manner. **The law is a convenience created to let man live in a reasonable society.***

To venerate it simply because it exists is nonsense.

— Jeff Cooper, *The Gargantuan Gunsite Gossip 2,* p.284

The primary source of America's ills is her rejection of the Natural Law. There are just Two Rules in life. Encapsulated by my colleague Rick Maybury in just 17 words:

❶ Do all you have agreed to do, and

❷ Do not encroach on other persons or their property.

The first Rule covers civil law; the second criminal law.

This is the law which the Apostle Paul spoke of in Romans Chapter 2 Verse 15 as being written in our hearts. Meaning, the capacity for Natural Law was issued to us as universal inventory, along with the rest of our vital organs.

It is in our very nature to recognize and wish to obey the Natural Law. This is why every major religion in history is in accord with those 17 words.

The Western world codified this over time and called it the Common Law. Common Law was the system for discovering and applying Natural Law in human affairs. I say "was the system" because it's been stolen from us. Since law contains the guidelines for the use of force, governments want control of these guidelines to make themselves exempt.

This is why governments hate the Common Law, and always nationalize the justice industry in order to implement their preferred system, Political Law. Our Government stole the Common Law and replaced it with legal positivism, in which the law is no better than the source of its authority.

mala en se crimes
mala prohibita "crimes"

In my novel *Molôn Labé!* is a chapter which dramatizes the trial of a peaceable man maliciously prosecuted by the US Government for a technical infraction of the gun laws. His defense attorney, Juliette Kramer, explains the two kinds of crimes during her closing argument:

"Folks, there is one crucial thing that Mr. Krempler from the United States Government failed to explain to all of us. It is vital to today's case."

"Mr. Krempler did not explain that there are two kinds of crimes. A few crimes are mala in se, which is Latin for 'evil in themselves.' These would be crimes of violence and property, such as murder, rape, and robbery. By the way, we've all heard that saying 'Ignorance of the law is no excuse' haven't we? Do you know where it came from? From an 18th century British legal scholar named Blackstone. His Commentaries on the Laws of England had an enormous influence on our jurisprudence. Blackstone wrote about ignorance of the law in this way: 'Ignorantia juris quod quisque tenetur scire, neminem excusat.' Translation: 'Ignorance of the law, which everyone is bound to know, excuses no man.'

"What is that law 'which everyone is bound to know'? Why mala in se crimes, of course. Everyone knows that it's wrong to murder, rape, and rob. Mala in se crimes are recognized in every state and in every nation as crimes, and they have been for thousands of years.

"So, what's been keeping our lawmakers busy since at least the War of 1812? Creating new and needless mala prohibita—wrongs prohibited. These 'crimes' are not evil in themselves, but merely

wrong because some group of politicians said that they're wrong. For example, that your backyard fence may not be over eight feet high, or that your home may not have rock landscaping. Or that recently imported rifles may not have muzzle attachments with a particular pattern of holes or slots. These mala prohibita—and there are tens of thousands of them—differ from city to city, from state to state, and from nation to nation. We've all heard examples of those old, silly laws still on the books, such as forbidding the whistling past a barbershop on Tuesdays. My client, Bill Russell has been tried under Title 18 of the US Code for such a 'crime.' He risks being convicted as a felon—a felon, ladies and gentlemen!—for a perfectly harmless metal part costing the price of lunch. 'Simon Says' that his muzzle brake cannot 'significantly reduce' muzzle flash. Whistling past a barbershop on Tuesday . . .

"Mr. Krempler will tell you that the law is not on trial, that we must all obey the law—even if it's a silly one—until we have persuaded our representatives to repeal it. Now that's fine reasoning for a fifth grade social studies class, but it doesn't quite hold water in the real world, does it?"

— from *Molôn Labé!* by Boston T. Party (2004), pp.26-27

Natural Law prohibits *mala en se* crimes
Political Law creates *mala prohibita* "crimes"

Even though the 2nd Amendment clearly states that your right to keep and bear arms *"shall not be infringed,"* (strong, unequivocal verbiage that no other Amendment enjoys), *mala prohibita* federal legislation has made illegal:

rifles too short	handguns too long
rifles too military-looking	guns too powerful
and all guns too quiet	

You'll go to jail if your gun has a muffler, and if your car does not. That is Political Law in action.

THE GOAL OF POLITICAL LAW

Mala prohibita legislation rules the land. Here's why:

By now it should be evident what the project of all laws that criminalize innocent conduct in order to prevent crime is: to so arrange the material conditions of life that those disposed to act upon their evil intentions will have no means of realizing their designs. Matters must be so arranged that, though criminals will want to use guns, they just won't be able to get them. People will want to use drugs, they just won't be able to buy them. Crazy people will want to blow up buildings; they just won't be able to. Thus will the world be made a safer place.

And now we come to the critical point, the self-destructive contradiction inherent in laws that criminalize innocent character to prevent crime before it occurs: their goal is to make responsibility irrelevant. It doesn't matter if criminals want to commit murder with guns; we will arrange things so that they simply cannot. Pass Brady and a few other well-crafted laws, vigorously enforce them, and it won't matter whether people act responsibly or not. Their irresponsible intentions will be rendered impotent and irrelevant.

(BTP NOTE: The same premise behind The Minority Report.*)*

Query: how does the law have the moral authority to hold people responsible for their behavior, if the law is engaged in a project whose operative presumption is that responsibility and irresponsibility can be made irrelevant, and are a matter of indifference? How do criminals, how does anyone, learn that they are responsible for actions, if the law is engaged in a mighty project to render it irrelevant whether one does or does not want to act responsibly?

And if we think that laws designed to prevent crime can indeed make the world a safer place, we should as ourselves this: How, exactly, is the world made a safer place by making self-control and responsibility irrelevant?

— Jeff Snyder, *Nation of Cowards* (2001), p.76-77

The goal of Political Law is not to punish *mala en se* crimes, but to eliminate the social need for morality and self-government. Why? Because an immoral and irresponsible electorate is what our modern political system has come to require. As H.L. Mencken so wisely quipped, an election is merely the advance auction of goods yet to be stolen. A moral and self-governing people will not participate in a system of institutionalized fraud, theft, plunder, and murder.

Hence, morality and self-government must *go*. By eliminating freedom (*i.e.*, the reward of responsible behavior), we eliminate the need for responsible behavior. Our Government no longer trusts us to act morally, and it doesn't matter socially if we *do* act morally. The so-called "zero-tolerance" basis of law enforcement requires no *mens rea* (evil intent). Exceed the speed limit, or sell a gun to a peaceable citizen in the next state and you've broken some *malum prohibitum* law. Never harmed anyone? "Doesn't *matter*. Just shut up and *comply*. It's the *law*."

THE PURPOSE OF THIS BOOK

First of all, I did *not* write *You & The Police!* for career scumbags who violate the Natural Law with *mala en se* crimes. Even if I *had,* such would be useless to them because they're either too dumb to use this book, or bright enough not to need it.

You & The Police! is for the honest citizen increasingly being caught in an increasingly totalitarian net.

Over the past twenty years I've grown outraged at this snowballing Draconianism. Thus, *You & The Police!* was born in 1996. It sold very well for eight printings (tied with my *Bulletproof Privacy*). Thousands of innocent readers are now no longer ignorant of their rights or police procedure. These educated Americans have denied the infant police state the one thing it still needs to operate: *cooperation.* Barring actual probable cause to arrest, the average soul has (with this book) little to fear from cops who overstep constitutional bounds.

Not that our job as constitutional citizens is getting any easier. Not with legislative travesties such as the *PATRIOT Act* of 2001, a 342 page monstrosity obviously written well before 9/11 and forced on an exiled Congress nervous about the anthrax scare. (How *convenient.*)

WHAT MAKES *ME* AN "EXPERT?"

Though I am no criminal, I have dealt with the police often. Why? I have a "leadfoot" and have been accosted by the "Radar Brownshirts" many, *many* times. (Scores of times, actually.) My attitude towards high-speed driving is *Autobahnian.* As long as one's driving is preponderantly safe under the conditions present, what difference does the exact *speed* matter? In fact, roughly one-quarter of the states will allow you to argue this very issue in court as your right to rebut the *prima facie* presumption that exceeding the posted limits is unsafe.

Any arbitrary speed limit so cautious to the point of absurdity (*e.g.,* 55 mph limits on highways designed to handle traffic at 80+) constitutes *theft* of my Life and Property (time) and Pursuit of Happiness—*highway robbery.* Enforcement of the vile 55/65 mph limit is primarily revenue-based, and thus greedy.

Traffic tickets are generally written for money, not for safety. (That is why many states will not even apply the infraction to your driving record if you pay an uncontested ticket early. It's only about the $.) It is *true* "highway robbery."

This stubborn fact, coupled with my personal animosity towards unreasonable restraints upon my mobility, explains my attitude regarding our ridiculous highway speed limits (the lowest in the Western world). Combined with my leadfoot and 20-40K of travel each year, I've spent dozens of roadside hours with police. I discuss all this so you'll know *why* I have so much non-arrest experience with the police, and thus how I presume to write authoritatively on this subject.

Do I like the police? Well, that *depends* . . .

I use the term "cops" throughout mainly because most police are *not* sworn officers. An "officer" is somebody who has a *sworn* oath of office to *"support this Constitution"* (as required in VI:3). We no longer have a sworn police force. Ask your local cop if s/he swore a constitutional oath of office. Today, cops generally work for *corporations* (cities, counties and States) as "security guards" to enforce largely corporate regulations (called *"code"*). "Police officers" would be misleading. Beyond that, I mean no disrespect by the term "cops"—that's what they call *themselves,* anyway.

Please, don't get me wrong here—I'm *not* against the police. Not as long as they behave as *sworn peace officers.* Peace officers are my friends, but when cops stomp around as "law enforcement" officers wearing black "ninja" suits and intrude upon harmless folks who in no way disturb the peace, they no longer have my support.

CORRECTING THE MODERN BULLY

Obviously, our most likely brush with the State is the traffic stop. It is clear that the 55 mph speed limit (a result of both Congressional extortion and State governors' timidity) and its demanded enforcement was the initial catalyst in the tragic transformation of our police (from reasonable peace officer to the modern revenue-based "law enforcement" officer).

The State cannot afford to roust *everyone*, so it must randomly flex its muscle on the passersby in a sort of "negative lottery." While on the road or going through airports and checkpoints, you are vulnerable to this spotty attention. *"Your papers!"* is the common "greeting," followed by a general probe of your activities. We must squash this East German attitude.

Since we've allowed such intrusion on the streets, it has now seeped into our private and business affairs. We've but a few years to chasten this nosy bully, while he is still theoretically correctable. Some say that it's already too late, and they may indeed be correct regarding larger cities. Big Brother is a well-established cosmopolitan dude, but he is still weak in the hinterlands and must rely upon the local *gendarmerie*—many of whom are still real peace officers.

Attitude is the vital thing!

I didn't write this book for the "sheeple." You know, those who bleat, *"If you've got nothing to hide, then you shouldn't object to a search of your stuff."* I wrote this book for you Americans who are horrified at the thought of warrantless searches of your property. I wrote it for the courageous who have properly armed themselves to protect their families amidst our savage society, regardless if such is technically illegal. (*"I'd rather be tried by twelve than carried by six."*)

Only *armed* people can be *free* people, and the State knows this. We must first be *disarmed* in order to be *enslaved*. This is an irrefutable historical constant. Every genocide in modern times was preceded by gun registration and confiscation. Much of the State's *future* oppression must and will deal with the coercive disarmament of individual Americans, face to face. Such will require a "National Emergency" (from a "wave of terrorism" or whatever) and subsequent legislation. *Then* there will be Troops-In-Your-Street.

We still have time to exercise Liberty

Overt martial law is probably imminent, but not for a few years. The State must first weed out those who cherish Liberty amongst the indoctrinated automata of enforcement (*e.g.*, the Would-You-Shoot-An-American-Gunowner survey given to US Marines at 29 Palms.)

The State must oppress within a framework of *perceived* law and justice, for if it doesn't the State will lose its vital popular support. Hence, you and I still have some good cards in our hand, and the State can only win through our own ignorance and fear. Our hand is still strong enough to make the State "fold" in a one-on-one game. Quit *believing* that the State always holds the winning hand. Learn your cards, and play them.

My personal philosophy is that one must constantly, without hurting others, seek the true boundaries and probe them. Find out where they are and see if they may be stretched. Life itself is a vast orchard of opportunity, yet 95% of people are self-incarcerated within their own mental hologram of desert corrals. *Everything* begins with, and thus ultimately rests upon, only *one* thing: your *vision*. See life as a desert corral, and a hot, dry, sandy, fly-ridden existence will be your reward. Instead of whining that others enjoy tropical fruit, why not see this life as the paradise it *can* be and get your *own* mangos?

What's my point? Don't allow others, *especially* the State to define or color your vision. There is Freedom to be had! Great pressures are in league to squeeze your Life and your Liberty into their manila folder for some bureaucratic filing cabinet—*resist!* A lack of information isn't the problem; a lack of *guts* is. **Get *scrappy!*** I realize it's like sweeping water uphill and you'll have little help, but the only alternative is the deluge. Grab a "broom" and get back to sweeping!

I've been on the "front lines" in the war for Liberty for some time now, and I want to train you how to win your own battles. **How *you* handle The Scene will make *all* the difference. *You* are the most important variable, not the cop.** *You* are the one who can turn bad into good and good into bad. This book, along with some courage, will keep all but the most outrageous oppression at bay. But you must first be committed to exercising whatever rights are still recognized.

Quit acting on fear. Fear is a poor long-term petrol, and an even worse chauffeur. Man or mouse?—decide now. To quote *The Shawshank Redemption*, *"Get busy living, or get busy dying."* If you're not a *victor,* then you're a *victim*—and thus, part of the problem. Once you've refused to be a victim to Big Brother, then you and I and others can start to rebuild a truly fair and just society based on the common law.

Learn to *win.* Slough off fear. Begin *now.*

❖ **2**

THE COP

Although today's cops are better trained and equipped, their basic nature is one of humanity's constants. Deep down, the cop is a simple animal—meaning, a creature of sniff and instinct. In short, a cop is a sort of *dog*. (I mean this *metaphorically,* not pejoratively.) He relies upon his ears, nose, teeth and growl. While some enjoy the actual fighting scrape, most prefer intimidation.

THE THREE KINDS OF COPS

The cop must be:

Over thirty-five years of age.
Completely competent in street law.
Of imposing presence.
In top physical shape, with emphasis on the ¼ mile and the hurdles.
Masterfully qualified in unarmed combat.
An expert motorist.
Able to hit what he shoots at.
Absolutely incorruptible.
Absolutely unflappable.
Multi-lingual.
Proud of his job.

Where can you find such a man, and for what wage?
— Jeff Cooper, *Gargantuan Gunsite Gossip 2,* (2001), p.141

I can help you during confrontations with one particular kind of cop. The other two are outside my book's scope.

The Good Cop ("GC")

is a *peace officer* and not a "law-enforcement officer." He is no zealous social reformer out to save you from yourself. Good Cop doesn't vigorously enforce unreasonable laws. He doesn't write a ton of needless speeding tickets. His attitude is, properly, *libertarian,* and he will not bother those who live peaceably. He supports the 2nd Amendment and has no qualms about honest, responsible folks carrying their own firearms. He knows that his authority derives from the People and he is mindful to be a good steward of that authority. He will neither try to trick you into a flimsy "consensual" search, nor bully you into waiving your rights or offering information about yourself. Good Cop is a treasure and should be actively supported. He's nearly all alone out there.

The Rogue Cop (The "RC")

is beyond reason. Knowing the law will rarely help when he is rousting you. Then and there, you can probably only fight or surrender. Either way, it won't be pretty.

Many federal agents are Rogue Cops. Backed by tremendous resources, a vast propaganda organ, and a hierarchy willing to usurp Liberty—these hyena packs seemingly get away with anything.

They get to wear black ninja suits and masks, kick in doors without announcement, terrorize old people for hours (DEA), shove pregnant women around into miscarrying (BATF), wantonly destroy private property (IRS, etc.), stomp family pets to death (again, BATF), shoot 13 y/o boys in the back on their own property (US Marshals at Ruby Ridge, Idaho), shoot mothers holding infants in the *face* with high-powered rifles (FBI sniper Lon Horiuchi at Ruby Ridge), gun you down if you mistake them as criminal band of marauders (DEA, etc.), and fill a homestead church with hundreds of CS gas cannisters—knowing full well that the 17 children inside *did not have gas masks* (FBI at Waco). Should you be treated with such a federal visit, this book will obviously be of little help.

The Intimidating Cop ("IC")

however, *is* the subject of *You & The Police!* He can still be "neutralized" on Scene with a firm, intelligent and polite stance. The State (at the *local* level) is still by-and-large Intimidating and not Rogue, as it recognizes a significant (though obviously dwindling) residual of inalienable rights.

As a personal political aside: I think that peace officers should be *drafted* into service for a brief stint of 12-18 months in exchange for their suffrage. **My point: anybody who *wants* to be a cop probably shouldn't be *allowed* on the force.** For the same reasons that we ought to have a citizen-soldiery and a citizen-Congress, we should have a citizen-police force which rotates back into "civilian" life. Citizen-cops would not cultivate this "us against them" philosophy and would not likely become robotic "law enforcement officers." Tyranny seems to be historically inevitable when a nation has succumbed to a system run by career politicians, career judges, career soldiers and career cops.

WINNING AGAINST AN "IC"

Don't fight an Intimidating State (lesser measures can work), and don't try to intimidate a Rogue State (you'll lose.)

But *how* to out-intimidate the Intimidating Cop? You *don't* do it by a growling contest, which only angers him. You see, he *believes* he's the Big Dog out there and the rest of us are puppies. He more than likely *became* a cop for the artificial power status, so he won't appreciate your challenge.

People are arrested for only *two* reasons: they broke the law and/or they angered the cop by transforming a generic scene into a *personal* thing. **Not creating a *personal* thing is paramount.** Being polite can get you off with a warning, while being a hothead jerk can get you arrested on any convenient pretext. Where no pretext exists, many IC's and most RC's will *create* such (resisting arrest, drugs "found" in your car, etc.).

The basis for intimidation is *bluff.* So, you don't try to out-bluff him, you win by subtly demonstrating that *you understand he's bluffing.* You *don't* blow up a bigger balloon than the cop's—you *deflate* his. "Blowing up a bigger balloon" (blustering about the law, or who you know, or threatening civil suits, etc.) turns the Scene into a personal matter and you absolutely *will not* win then and there, even if you're right and he's wrong. So, therein lies the trick—how to deflate his bluff balloon without overtly threatening his fragile Ego?

And now for a bit of psychology...

You want the scenario to turn into a deflated balloon in his hands, without him fully realizing when or understanding how it happened. The air simply left his balloon of bluff without a sound. It's like psyching out a snarling dog: you want him bewildered why his tough act didn't turn you into jelly. Properly done, he'll give a confused snort and back off.

It's accomplished by superior knowledge, unflappability, and dignified politeness. Not snobbery, mind you—cops hate a snob almost as much as a hothead. You want to portray an unconcerned assurance, like someone coolly taking on a winning bet. **You want to create Doubt in his mind.** I'm speaking of the Confidence of Power. Cops respect Power, and they know that there are higher powers than their badge.

Assuming that you're truly innocent of any real crime, all the cop can do is cause you some minor inconvenience. If he does, *and you know the law*, you can cause him some major legal headaches. You want him to understand that: ❶ You're not a criminal, and ❷ If he mistakenly treats you as one you will obtain ample legal recourse. Done well, 95+% of the IC's (and perhaps 80% of the RC's) will want you to go away.

I can teach you the basic techniques, but success requires that *you* can pull it off. Many people cannot: they're Nervous Nellies, or they're perennial hotheads, or they're devious ("hinky" in coptalk).

The Intimidating Cop's weakness

His biggest weakness is that he is usually bluffing. He is standing in the air and assumes you *believe* he's on the ground. He likes to appear taller than he is because his real height is below average. Not content with honest self-achievement, and reaching eye-level with the productive world, he became a cop for its exalted position of artificial authority. It's based on little more than his gun and the guns of his buddies, and deep down in his canine-like brain, he *knows* it. His gun, unlike the fully-flowered bully Rogue Cop, is more bark than bite. Intimidating Cop has neither the mature self-esteem to be Good Cop, nor the stupid testosterone to be Rogue Cop.

Intimidating Cop's weakness is his own little *self.* Inside his bluff, he's naked. You must cleverly expose his nakedness. He will then want only for you to go away. **You've made his goal coincide with your own,** *and that's the idea!*

Specifically, IC is not only unsure of himself, but unsure of the *State.* Why? Because the State, the fountainhead of his supposed power, is unsure of itself. Since Americans still enjoy *some* rights and freedoms, the State must often tread lightly through a legal and procedural maze. The State is not *yet* as encompassing as Nazi Germany; it *does* have a few boundaries. These boundaries are very much in judicial flux (as are, conversely, our rights) and this makes the eager State nervous. A nervous State makes for a nervous cop, except for Rogue Cop, who is usually too far gone to be nervous.

But IC *is* nervous. He's not a lawyer. He doesn't even have a legalistic mind. So, what *does* he know about the law? Only what he's been briefed on. He was issued a legal handbook, compiled by the State's AG office and done in three-ring notebook. New case law is handed down every month regarding stops, arrests, searches and seizures. Where do these cases come from? From IC's and RC's pushing things too far.

Your IC could be the *next* **case history, and he** *knows* **this.** But he doesn't automatically know that *you* know this. And that's *your* duty—to subtly inform him that *you* understand the dynamic boundaries, his risks and his potential costs. You want him to gradually realize that pushing a nonexistent issue with you and thereby violating your rights will gain him nothing but professional embarrassment and expense. You want him to arrive at his *own* conclusion that he'd be much better off letting you on your way.

The IC's fears

The flip side to his insecurities is fear—that he will be found out to be small, inferior, and inconsequential.

Affront to his reputation and ego

Nothing stings an IC or RC worse than to be embarrassed by his own dumb mistake or overreaction. His Power Image amongst the public and his Status amongst peers is *everything*.

Cops gossip more than old hairdressers, and to lose face is nearly intolerable. I know of a couple of great stories:

The first one comes from *Police Sniper* by Craig Roberts. Back in the 1950's and 60's when America preferred its cops as big and bright as Buicks, one such cop responded to an old lady's call about a wild animal in her basement. As a precaution against a rabid critter, Big Cop ventured downstairs with his shotgun, to discover her cat backed into a corner by a large raccoon. Big Cop blasted the raccoon. The old lady, terrified, screamed from the doorway, *"What happened?"* Big Cop told her that he had blown away the raccoon. *"Well, what about my cat?"* she asked. Big Cop shrugged and replied, *"Gee, lady—if you say so!"* and blew away her cat, too.

The second story involves a CHP who pulled over an extremely frazzled mother with a car full of kids. It was a hot summer day, the kids were howling like scalded banshees, and now she's getting this speeding ticket. Her disposition, predictably, was rather sour. The CHP, annoyed with her attitude, said something like, *"Gee, lady, what's your problem? Is it your time of the month or something?"* At that she utterly snapped and punched him out. I don't mean punched him, I mean flat knocked him *out cold*, right there on the highway!

Obviously, neither of these cops ("Whiskers" and "Kotex," presumably) will *ever* live this down!

Departmental reprimand and suspension

A bad enough incident could jeopardize future promotions or have him reassigned into a dead-end department.

Adverse media attention

If this is sufficiently intense and unrelenting, many PD's will toss him overboard to save the overall image.

Lawsuits

A very remote, though real, threat. Many arrested suspects swear to sue, but few actually do. Even if a damaged party is serious about suing, it requires the DA to go along, and even if *that* happens, the case takes years to reach trial.

PREPARING YOUR PERSON

There are two reasons to prepare your own person: ❶ to avoid being detained or arrested; and ❷ to avoid digging a deeper hole for yourself if you *are* frisked during a detention or searched during an arrest. *Preparation* is the key here, as you won't have the physical opportunity or cold presence of mind *during* a confrontation to improve your situation. Plan ahead for a worst case arrest scenario.

Have *no* outstanding warrants for your arrest

I'm not talking about felonies and crimes of violence—those people *should* be arrested. What I mean are unresolved parking and traffic tickets. While it is tempting to let such slide since the cops rarely come to your door for these minor matters, *don't.* They'll surface at the very worst moments, like on the way to the airport to catch a flight. (When I was much younger, it took me a couple of times to learn this, the *hard* way.) If your freedom is important to you, then pay up and keep your *"Status Clear."* You must be able to survive a computer check, which today is quite encompassing—even nationally, if need be.

Keep incriminating stuff off your person

This is not advice for *real* criminals guilty of *mala in se* (evil in themselves) crimes. It is intended for harmless, peaceable folk who may run afoul of various bureaucratic *mala prohibita* (wrongs prohibited).

Carry a pager *and* large amounts of cash (*i.e.*, over Ø1,000) and this betokens drug dealing.

Keep helpful information to the cops off your person

This is trickier, as we need to carry with us the paper jumble of modern life: appointment book, credit cards, phone numbers, "to do" lists, receipts (which precisely locate you in time and place), business cards, video rental cards, discount coupons, etc. These items are obviously useful to us. They're also useful to the officials, especially if they've taken an unusually keen interest in you. Such personal and timely information speaks volumes of your habits and associations—information which would otherwise be extremely difficult to obtain. (Go through your wallet right now and imagine what would be known about you if such were found.)

So, how to eat your cake and have it, too?

Palmtop Digital Assistant (PDA)

The solution which has worked well for *me* is a PDA. Roughly 3"x6"x½" and $100-300, it can hold many *megs* of personal data. PDAs today are as powerful as desktop computers were back in the late 1980s. They have a powerful operating system (OS) which will support PGP. (Very soon we will see wireless PDAs begin to replace cell phones.) Palm Pilot and Handspring are the two major brands.

All of these palmtops offer password protection; meaning there's a public area and a secret area. Any unauthorized person trying to have a peek would be barred from the secret area. In fact, the only thing I put in the public area is a *"Cash Reward if found!"* note with a relative's phone number, so at least the unit has a chance of making it back to me if lost. (An even better idea is to buy a tag from www.stuffbak.com, and register with an alias email from a public computer. Then, the authorities don't have a traceable reward phone number for you.)

If your unit allows up to, say, 30 characters for your passphrase, then use all 30 to increase the time and difficulty of breaking through. (*Never* write down the passphrase!) While I am not a computer hacker, these units seem to me fairly secure. I do not know if they are generally built with a password "backdoor," but one model of mine needed factory repair, and, as a test, I claimed to have lost my password (hoping they would admit to a "backdoor"). They honestly appeared to be stumped, so I "found" my password (in order that they could save my data). If any of you have solid information of the existence of password "backdoors" on PDAs, please let me know.

Even if your PDA *were* taken and compromised, there is no handwriting or fingerprint evidence on the data itself, so the data may be disavowed, if you choose. Pay for the thing with cash, leave no traceable name for warranty purposes, and nobody can *prove* that you bought it, much less filled it with any particular data. If all this seems too clandestine or even "paranoid," remember (or learn firsthand) that times are serious and Liberty is quite endangered.

After you become proficient on your PDA you'll find little need for paper notes. Any notes I *do* make on paper are mere cryptic, shorthand abbreviations. Regarding other "helpful information," for example, there's no reason to have on your person: airline tickets days before your flight, business cards and phone numbers which have already been entered in your PDA, "to do" lists, schedules, receipts (which pinpoint your location in date/time), etc.

Your PDA can be backed up on computer and the files encrypted. Also, you can backup on a small RAM chip. Either way, keep your data somewhere other than home or office.

Think of it this way: what would *your* personal papers tell the police about you if you were for some reason suddenly arrested. I posed this same question to myself many years ago after being hauled in for an old speeding ticket (which my attorney claimed to have "fixed"). Among my effects were a handwritten address book with 400+ names (this was B.P.—Before Palmtops), travel schedule, etc. All of it *could* have been easily photocopied (but wasn't) and used against me at some later date. It was a lesson I've never forgotten. Keep your personal info *private*—don't be your own enemy.

The value of "fanny packs"

What's great about fanny packs is: ❶ they'll hold all your personal effects, including palmtop, pager or cell phone; and ❷ they are quickly removable to lock in a briefcase or trunk. (By contrast, try discreetly emptying all your pockets while being pulled over.)

If a fanny pack does not mesh with your style, use a lockable briefcase or bag. A locked container is still a fairly solid legal barrier against most general snooping. The police will need probable cause to search it, as I'll later describe.

Have *only* these essentials on your person

If pulled over, the only things to have on you are:

license/registration/insurance,
AAA bond card, or sufficient bail cash for any likely fine
some pocket change to make phone calls
micro digital voice recorder,
your lawyer's card
a second car door key hidden on you (or on the car)

Your other keys should be on a detachable ring and hidden in your car. (If asked to open your trunk, refuse and reply that you misplaced the key, anyway.) *Only* these things do you need then, and *only* those things should you have on you. Everything else should be locked in a briefcase, a hard case, and/or locked in the trunk.

❖ 4

BEFORE GETTING
IN YOUR CAR

There are many overlapping physical preparations you should make before entering the hostile environment called *"in public."* Properly done, you'll reduce your chance of a bogus search or arrest by 95%. But you must do these things *in advance*—consistently. In rough sequential order:

Car preparations to make in advance
What I'm going to outline may seem extreme, but it's best to plan for a baseless search and/or arrest. While *You & The Police!* is for the peaceable American, you may someday become enmeshed in a nasty confrontation with the police. By protecting yourself with legal knowledge and practical preparations *before* this happens, you will greatly minimize the unpleasant outcome—possibly eliminating it altogether.

Have a locked strongbox bolted to the trunk floor
Such proves your *"heightened expectation of privacy"* while offering some protection against both car burglars and police searches gone overboard. Army surplus stores often have sturdy, steel cases for ammo and equipment. The .50 caliber ammo cans are $6 and will hold a couple of pistols and ammo. The 20mm and 30mm cannon round boxes are much larger and very affordable at $20.

Whichever you choose, take it to a good welder for him to attach some locking hardware (or even *build* you a box). Ideally, he should construct a steel shroud surrounding the lock and hasp. The lock should be a brass Sesame or Master 4-dial combination (which eliminates the need for a vulnerable key). Use at least 3/8ths inch Grade 4 bolts with Nylok nuts and *big* washers to secure the box in your trunk or truck bed. Attach them upside-down with the bolt head underneath the floor.

What goes in your strongbox? Anything you don't want easily stolen, confiscated, or snooped through: pistols, ammo, cash, personal papers, etc. The police will need probable cause (PC) to search such a strongbox.

Create a "trunk" if your car doesn't have one

If the interior of your car is entirely open (as in vans and station wagons), its entirety is vulnerable to a *Terry* frisk since the whole *car* would probably be considered within your *"immediate control."* This is discussed fully in Chapter 7.

Small station wagons and hatchbacks often have a "privacy shelf" which rises and lowers with the rear door. If your car hasn't such a shelf, you should construct one to preclude (as with a trunk) any possibility of interior access to the rear.

Vans are more problematical. An interior wall behind the cab is required to separate the passenger compartment from the cargo area. Any door should be openable only from the back.

Take photos of your secured areas

Photos prove, not only the structural details, but your *"heightened expectation of privacy."* This will also help disprove any false assertion that you consented to a search. Since you want the police to resort to physically breaking in such a strongbox, photos of its pristine condition are vital.

Make sure that your door locks without a key

Many modern cars don't allow this, so to prevent the driver from negligently locking himself out. While nice for the absentminded, you do not (or *should* not) need this. As explained later, when being pulled over you'll want to be able to get out of your car and close the locking door behind you, without a key.

Remove the inside door panel. Operate the lock with the key to locate which connecting arm to disable. (If stumped, remove the passenger door panel to compare the internal difference. Passenger doors are lockable without the key.)

Car key preparations

First, you *don't* want to use the original car key. You'll wear it out or break it, necessitating a replacement from the locksmith. Use your original key solely as a *master* to make copies—as with software disks. **Use copies, *not* the master!**

The copies should be utterly *generic,* without factory logos. Generic copies are not only cheaper, but if searched as a pedestrian your car keys will not immediately convey the make of your car. I do this whenever I have a rental car, for privacy, and to use the master key as a hidden spare.

Many, if not most, cars today use one key for everything: doors, glovebox, and trunk. While obviously convenient, it makes your trunk easily violated by mechanics, valet parking, and by the police. The more the cops must actually break into your property during a search, the more likely that the search will be found *"unreasonable"* and thus improper, and the more leverage you will have against them in a lawsuit. When exiting the car during a stop, your trunk key should be hidden inside the car—*not* on your person.

Buy a trunk lock and key from a salvage yard for 25-50% of the new price. Make sure that the lock is in good, operating condition and that the key works.

Combination lock gas cap with internal key compartment

This is the neatest thing I've found in years. Your spare keys are protected, and without a vulnerable key on your person. I thought about putting in some emergency currency, but gasoline does soak the compartment.

My cap was a mail order gift. I wish I had a source for you, but if you ask around enough you'll find one.

Paperwork to have inside your car

This goes beyond registration and insurance, if you're so required. If you've recently paid off a speeding ticket or, better yet, got it dismissed, keep a copy of the receipt or court disposition in your car. Computer errors abound, given the sloppy nature of traffic court personnel, and I've found it extremely helpful to be able to *prove* at roadside a bench warrant to be erroneous. While you might even still be arrested, you could later allege bad faith on the part of the cop. AAA bail bond cards are also incredibly handy to have.

BTP idea: dedicated in-car cell phone camera

Most cop cars have a dashboard video camera. You can, too. A cell-phone camera installed on the passenger's A-pillar will capture both you and the officer in conversation. Make sure that your hands are visible for a nonthreatening posture.

The cellular uplink is vital. If the data were simply stored in your car, a search would find it and why tempt a cop from erasing it? They have often confiscated and erased arrestee's cassette recordings when it suited them. Have the signal transmitted somewhere safe, such as to your lawyer's office or a trusted friend. (If you have a network of like-minded people, somebody could serve as the group receiver/archivist for this.)

The system should have its own battery, and be well-hidden to survive against routine *Terry* frisks, searches incident to arrest, and inventory searches. (Little, however, can survive against a full-blown *French Connection* search for drugs.)

This is your insurance policy against an erroneous arrest and search. Do not warn the roadside cop that you have this system, else he won't incriminate himself. (A very sly cop may even find a way to circumvent or defeat it.) Suffer through any Scene you must, because you will have his career in your hands, if not a very large civil suit settlement as well.

Once you use such a recording, the word *will* be out about your system. Expect to be thereafter left alone . . . or *not*.

Other misc. stuff to have in your car

A radar detector is *vital* these days. Enforcement of speed limits (especially on the highways) is more for *revenue* than safety purposes. Europeans travel at 80+ mph on highways twice as congested as ours with a fourth of fatalities proportionally. Speeding tickets mean big bucks. Don't be a "winner" of this "negative lottery." Good radar detectors alerting to X, K, Ka photo radar, and laser bands can be had for under Ø100. Mine pays for itself every month.

Have a combination lock briefcase next to you. It's roomy and secure, yet innocuous. You can disarm, legally and effectively, within seconds, as I'll describe in a few pages.

Have a digital voice recorder with you to tape a Scene going sour. (Mine has squelched two particularly bad Scenes. The cops knew I was serious.) If you're *really* intent about thwarting a nasty Scene, then you should have installed a digital cell phone camera.

Don't give the cops a *single* reason to stop you

Make sure your car's plate (whatever it is) is up to date and can withstand a computer check. (Those hardy souls using Sovereign-based Right-To-Travel plates should expect to be stopped, often—and their cars occasionally impounded. While I admire their daily courage, it's a tough battle, and I've seen very few victories.)

Have no glaring equipment faults (broken headlight or taillight, loud exhaust, bald tires, etc.). Many criminals were *originally* pulled over for the classic cracked windshield. **Remember, cops work for the State and the State is in search of *bodies.*** The Scene first requires that you've drawn attention to yourself. Check out your car as a pilot checks out his airplane. Pretextual traffic stops with *"reasonable suspicion"* or *"probable cause"* are now permitted by the Court.

Remove political and philosophical bumper stickers, or you may offend the cop for no good purpose. (This was personally difficult for me, as I cherish a rich bumper sticker. As witty as *"If It Weren't For Guns, You'd Be A British Subject"* is, you don't want to enrage the wrong cop.) As "Chairman" Mao said, *"Move through the masses like a fish through water."* Gee, even Commies sporadically have good advice . . .

Your car's interior should be *clean* and nearly empty

As the courts have said, *"The eye cannot commit a trespass."* Not only will a clean, empty interior discourage petty thievery, it offers less to the cop in *"plain view"* and reduces his time and interest at the Scene.

Check under the seats for old beer bottles or shell casings which will always roll out at the worst time. Do not have controversial literature strewn about. Ditto for extreme forms of music. (Inside my car I have utterly no papers, letters, or books visible—a real *tabula rasa.* Very little can be gleaned about me from my car interior.) Radar detectors should be hidden as cops hate them. (Also, keep your car *clean.* If you *look* like a dirtbag, you'll be *treated* as one.) Make sure the dashboard VIN is visible.

Look like a polite, law-abiding *"Yes, Sir!"* type

Sprinkling about a couple of tension-reducing items is helpful: a toy or two if you have children (or better yet, a babyseat); textbooks if you're in school, etc. **Don't, however, overdo it!** A hint, a whiff, a mere suggestion is all you need to pass as "Joe College" or "Bob Family Man." On this note, *"Say No To Drugs"* and *"Sheriff's Association Member"* stickers are too overt and often make the cop suspect that you're trying too hard to *appear* law-abiding. As I said, don't overdo it. Cops are good at detecting the *too* obvious. Too much of a "white flag" can easily be a "red flag"—know what I mean?

Have no drugs or residue in your car/on your person

Obviously. Life is greatly simplified when drugs are absent. This is especially true regarding You and the State.

The federal courts have held (mistakenly, in my view) that a dog sniff doesn't first require *"probable cause"* (PC) because such isn't technically a *"search"* under the 4th Amendment. Well, *that's* neat. The *"plain smell"* doctrine applies also to dogs, and their alerting to drugs creates PC. (Some states may, happily, have more restrictive rules on dog sniffs.)

In *my* view, anything beyond a human's senses is a *"search."* Whenever a cop's 5 senses are amplified through the use of *any tool* (binoculars, parabolic microphone, X-ray, a dog's nose, etc.), seems a *"search"* within the meaning of the 4th. But that's *me*. (The Court recently denied use of thermal imagers without a warrant. They throw us a bone sometimes.)

So, the police were provided with a neat loophole—the drug-sniffing dog. From my understanding, the dog is tough to beat. If you are carrying drugs, and the cop is suspicious enough to call for a dog, you *will* be sniffed and found out. Those who smoke pot regularly will carry enough smell on their body and clothes to alert a dog, even if they've no pot in their car (or *your* car). Bummer, dude.

Worse yet, even if you've never used drugs, the dog will likely alert to the smell left behind by a passenger, mechanic, or former owner of your car. If you buy a used car, have it *thoroughly* steamcleaned and deodorized. Check in seatcracks, and underneath the seats for an old "roach." Threaten to horsewhip anyone who brings so much as drug *residue* into your car.

If you have friends who use illegal drugs, explain the foolish risks to you. Once a cop has PC for drugs on a passenger, the entire car is subject to search, including your belongings.

If you're in *their* home or car, you'll probably pick up enough of a residue to later alert a drug dog, so be careful. Also, you might be there if *they* get busted. If so, you *will* be detained and frisked—maybe even arrested and searched.

Lock ALL other items in the trunk

If you don't *absolutely* need it on the road, stow it in the trunk. Contents in your trunk are not within your *"immediate control"* are immune from a **Terry** frisk and *"search incident to arrest."* Full-blown PC is necessary to search there.

If not carried on/about your person, firearms should not only be unloaded and in the trunk—but in a locked container. Ditto for personal papers. That way, in case an IC gets in your trunk he is then thwarted by additional locked containers. (I read about a druggy who had a small *safe* in his trunk. Upon arrest, the cops seized his safe (for "inventory purposes") but couldn't crack it before the druggy was sprung. Druggy got back his unopened safe. Sometimes even dirtbags have some clever moves. I say: Learn where and when you can. Or, everybody *else's* stuff is grist for *my* mill.)

Totally benign items such as shopping bags, etc. should also be stored in the trunk. Reason being, such is *information.* If the local SEARS was just robbed and the bandit escaped in a car similar to yours, the cop who is now writing you a speeding ticket might think he's actually busted the creep because of the SEARS bag on the seat. Far fetched? Yeah, maybe—however, I wouldn't take *any* chances. **You want to give the cop nowhere to go.** Keep your car a real *tabula rasa* which connotes/implies *nothing.* It could be a vital edge . . .

Secure your personally carried firearm

In open-carry states, I often do so. (Sometimes, I even exit the car wearing my pistol if stopped, though this is increasingly a bad idea.) Such is perfectly lawful. I do not swagger or bluster because of my pistol—in fact, I act as if it doesn't exist. If he brings it up, I stress that *I'm on his side*, that I take gun bearing very seriously and do *not* carry to intimidate the public. Interestingly, in the four times I've been stopped in open-carry states for speeding, I was thrice let off with a polite warning. (One Good Cop engaged me in pleasant conversation and actually gave me a mini *salute* when we parted!) My impression over the years is that *most* (though not all) cops respect the courteously armed.

Most states, however, do *not* honor the 2nd Amendment and prohibit the open carry of firearms. Concealed carry, if allowed at all, is by permit only. So, what to do if pulled over in a non-open carry state? You must have a quick, subtle and foolproof way to unload and secure your gun *while being pulled over*. **Quick**—less than 15 seconds. **Subtle**—with no obvious body movement. **Foolproof**—defendable against a frisk.

I recommend a combination lock briefcase, left closed (but unlatched) on the passenger seat or floor. If you need to get your gun, it takes only a few seconds. However, when being pulled over, quickly and discreetly unload your gun, lock the ammo in the glovebox or some *sealed* container (it's best to have the ammo *separate* from the gun and mag, and *not* in the same container), put the gun in the briefcase, close and spin the dials. Your gun is neither loaded nor *"on or about the person"* and therefore you are no longer armed by general legal definition.

In this condition, if asked if I have a gun in the car, I'd say, *"I don't have to answer such personal questions."* All he can do in response is *Terry* frisk you and your car interior (though not locked containers or the trunk), which will find nothing.

Even if he later (legally or illegally) broke into your briefcase, you are still protected under the *McClure-Volkmer Act of 1986* which provides a federal "umbrella" for gunowners during interstate transit. As long as your gun is legal where you live and legal where you're going, states in between (such as Neu Jersey) can't arrest you if your guns are unloaded and cased. Even if the cops illegally break in your briefcase, the cops will illegally come up with zip (unless your gun was listed in the National Crime Index Computer (NCIC) as stolen). Illegally coming up with zip is a bad thing for the cop. You'll have grounds to sue him.

My briefcase trick is worth the price of this book. You'll be able to draw it quickly, or secure it quickly, depending on the situation. I do this on long trips through Occupied Territory with stringent gun laws.

If time were too short, I would simply remove the mag, clear the chamber, toss all in the case and lock it. That's at least better than nothing, and the cops wouldn't know it was even in there unless they broke into your case.

Don't practice this during the Scene—you'll be too nervous to do it well. Practice this with a friend watching from behind your car. You must be able to do this smoothly, or else the cop will get suspicious.

Good advice is worthless if you don't heed it! A reader friend of mine understands this now. He got stopped for speeding in draconian Ohio, and the cop saw his belt mag pouch. Immediate frisk/arrest/search/impound. They didn't at all care for his two handguns, a battle rifle, hundreds of rounds of ammo, and *sword*. (Nice touch, that.) All that and his laptop were confiscated and held for months. He was unfairly made to look odd and dangerous in the media. Verizon fired him. Fortunately, the DA chose not to prosecute the *felony* charge of unlicensed concealed carry, and a misdemeanor plea bargain was worked out after several thousand dollars in legal fees.

Jordan quipped that it wasn't a defeat, but a *"damn fine fighting retreat."* I blandly agree, **but *all* of this would have been *avoided* had he used my briefcase tip!** I say this not to gloat or bludgeon, but to show you how easy it is to get *sloppy* even when you know better.

Any highway stop can turn into a negative lottery. Stay sharp and don't skimp on your precautions. Whether you drive away or are driven away will mostly depend on how well you prepared yourself in advance. There's no time to remove belt mag pouches and holsters when you get pulled over. (That's why I like fanny packs for road trips.) Watch yourself on interstate trips! Occupied Territory is fraught with danger.

Your car should be able to withstand a **Terry** frisk at minimum. Meaning, anything remotely sensitive (*e.g.,* military-pattern rifles, bulk ammo, other weapons, certain books, etc.) should be kept only in a locked hard case.

Some final thoughts on preparation

This sums up the physical preparations you *should* have made and practiced *before* the Scene. I fully realize that the totality of these preparations seems rather extreme, but *without* such the Scene itself can *easily* become extreme—especially if you reserve your rights, refuse consent of a search, etc. **Trust me on this. It's the sum of the *little*** *things* **which count.** It's the *little things* which separate the amateur from the professional, the victim from the victor. **Remember,** *all the mistakes have already been made*—so **why do any of us need to reinvent the square wheel?**

I've watched countless episodes of *Cops* and the like, read hundreds of crime novels and legal cases, all the while asking myself, *"How did this guy blow it? Where was he his own enemy? When did the cops bluff because of the guy's ignorance?"*

Once detained (or worse, arrested) you will *not* have much (if any) freedom to directly improve your situation. You must play the cards you dealt yourself *before* the red lights flashed. Think of the above as insurance. Buy it now for later. The rest is mental preparation, a bit of confidence, and experience.

In your car, going down the road
In short, don't draw attention to yourself

Do not travel at outrageous speeds or flagrantly disregard safety laws. Wear your seat belt. (Yeah, I know it's hilarious fun to drive 95 mph, drinking beer, steering with your feet, throwing litter out the sunroof—but *cool* it!) If it's rude, it's probably illegal. Look and act like prosperous middle-class.

About speeding, at some point such is automatically considered to be *"reckless driving"*—usually 25mph or more in excess of the posted limit (states vary on this) and is at least a full-blown misdemeanor. If you travel a fast clip, be aware of when *"reckless driving"* kicks in your state, which means an instant arrest and your car impounded.

A last bit of advice

Take care that these precautions as a visual *whole* do not ironically attract attention. You don't want such precautions to be obvious, or even visible—so have your strongbox in the trunk vs. the rear passenger floor.

Therefore, do what is *reasonable* in your situation. Think your strategy through, be coolheaded and deliberate. Don't get all freaked out in advance. It's highly unlikely that anyone is out to get you personally.

Just don't draw attention to yourself by being *too* clever.

❖ **5**

NEVER CONSENT!

This will be the shortest and, ironically, the most important chapter of *You & The Police!* Many folks I spoke with expressed no small surprise at my recommended firm posture with the police. As you might have already gathered, I do not advise *any* kowtowing or compromising during the Scene.

"But you were the one who needlessly aggravated the whole deal!" many remarked after hearing my "war stories." Assuming a short-term perspective to be paramount, they're right—my intransigence *did* cost me time and inconvenience. For *me,* however, mere momentary convenience is rarely paramount. In police confrontations I take the *long* view.

During the Scene, cops rely upon the public's overwhelming desire to have the confrontation end. Most people will, in the hope of speeding up a cop's exodus, divulge, consent, placate, whatever—*anything* to make him go away. While this wimpy expediency can sometimes work to that effect, you may instead further confirm the cop's suspicions, or even give him probable cause to arrest you.

For example: By voluntarily surrendering ID during a mere contact, he could discover some unpaid ticket and warrant for your arrest. By offering your prior whereabouts you could unknowingly place yourself at the scene of some crime. By admitting association with certain persons you could drop yourself into their legal mess. One never knows.

I've said this before, and I'll say it again: **Cops work for the State and the State is in search of *bodies!*** The police exist to arrest criminals. During *any* confrontation with the police, there is at least *some* risk that *you* could be arrested. Remember, they wouldn't be talking to *you* in the first place unless *you* were somehow a potential "customer."

Fish are caught only because they opened their mouths! Keep yours *shut!*

I'm not saying that cops are always, or even generally, our adversaries, but they *can* be during any Scene. It's one thing to assist the police in catching criminals by giving information, but *watch out* when they start asking about *your* activities. My rule is not to discuss with officials anything related to myself. I do not answer personal questions, and I *never* consent to a requested search of my property.

If a cop asks to search your property, all sorts of warning bells should go off. Understand this: **There is *never* any real advantage to a consented search. Always, always, *always* refuse consent.** I don't mean often, or usually—I mean *always!* If you learn nothing else but *this* from my book, you'll probably fare well.

"Why not let me search if you're innocent and have nothing to hide?" a cop may taunt. A good reply is, *"Well, if you thought I were innocent, you wouldn't be interested in me."*

"Well, I can get a warrant!" the cop may menacingly retort. You should reply, *"I doubt it. Warrants are based on probable cause, and since I haven't done anything wrong there can be no probable cause of any crime. Good day, Officer."*

Walk away, close the door—shut down The Scene. (I'll show you exactly how in Chapters 6, 7, and 8.)

❖ **6**

THE CONTACT

There are three kinds of scenarios between you and the police: *contact/encounter, stop/detention, and arrest/custody.* Listed in order of severity, they require increasing amounts of crime-related evidence to be upheld. More is required to detain than to contact, more to arrest than to detain, and more to convict than to arrest.

Evidence vs. Restraint Triangle

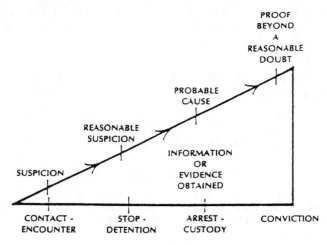

The object of my book is to teach you to recognize this progression of lawful restraint and how to "nip in the bud" any police confrontation you might have *at the lowest level possible.* The information required to do so increases at each successive stage, as do the risks. I could *give* away the mere pamphlet needed for the contact stage, like on changing the oil in your car.

However, for you to defuse the next stage (detention) requires *much* more information. This would be like giving your car a full tune-up. Arrests I'll leave for Chapter 9.

THE CONTACT / ENCOUNTER

This is consensual conversation between a cop and a private individual who can walk away or ignore the cop's questions. **While this seems innocent enough, always remember that cops are *never* truly "off duty."** I don't have a general problem with that, as criminals are never truly "off duty," either. Happily, most criminals are astoundingly stupid liars. Well knowing this, cops make effortless small talk with suspects to uncover *"probable cause."*

It's amazing what cops discover simply by asking. A retired California deputy told me about a kid on a bicycle with bulging pockets. Making simple contact, he asked, *"Hey, what's in your pockets?"* Instead of brushing off the question, the kid replied, *"My stash!"* *"Really, wow! Can I see?"* The little genius then pulled out several ounces of pot. Moral: to the cop it never hurts to ask, and it's never illegal, either.

Legal basis for the contact / encounter

No suspicion is required for a cop to merely contact you.

> There is nothing in the constitution which prevents a policeman from addressing questions to anyone on the streets.
> — *Terry v. Ohio,* 392 US 1 (1968); concurring opinion

Also, contacts made during a cop's "caretaking" capacity:

> ...arise from the police officer's duty to maintain peace and security, to protect citizens from harm or annoyance and to do all those innumerable tasks which society calls upon police to do.
> — *Batts v. Superior Court,* 100 Cal. Rptr. 181 (1972)

The above case arose when a cop knocked on a van door late at night to warn the occupants inside about the town's ordinance against sleeping in cars. Batts (rocket scientist in a former life) opened the van door exposing a pot party in progress, complete with pipe and weed in plain view. Such evidence was admissible, as no detention had occurred (which *would* have required *"reasonable articulable suspicion"*).

Your rights during a contact

Nearly total. You have the utter right to ignore him and walk away. Simple. You are not required to tell him your name, much less provide ID.

The cop's powers during a contact

Nearly zero. If you disengage, there's *nothing* he can do without the required *"reasonable articulable suspicion"* for detention or *"probable cause"* for arrest. He can, however, walk along with you in public and observe.

He *does* have, however, the power, during *any* kind of confrontation with you, to frisk you for weapons *if* : he has a reasonable belief that you are armed *and* that you pose a threat to him or the public. **He cannot *routinely* frisk *everyone* he contacts, or even detains.** He must first have reasonable belief of a threat based on articulable facts (***Terry v. Ohio,*** 392 US 1 (1968)). The so-called *Terry* frisk is limited to the patting down of clothing for weapons. He cannot reach into pockets for objects clearly not weapons.

He can most likely prohibit you from having your hands in your pockets (***People v. Ross,*** 265 Cal.Rptr. 921 (1990)). As a legal rule of thumb, the cop's *"reasonable"* perception of his safety will nearly always override your Constitutional rights.

The realities during a contact

Don't *believe* he's only being friendly—it's a fishing expedition. **Cops chat up people like guys chat up chicks.** We're talking ulterior motive, here. Don't be like some buxom, yet naïve, 15 y/o girl. He's not interested in your love of grandma and puppy dogs.

I've conversed with many cops. As I am a clean-cut, lawful type, I rarely tweak their antennae, so our talks have usually been benign and friendly. *Usually.* When they weren't, and I knew much less, I still managed to avoid any real hassle because of my innocence and innate righteous indignation.

This was a crutch until I became more wise to the Scene and how to defuse it. Today, however, there is no time for you to learn all this the *slow* way. You need a crash course, and this book is it.

Practical tips during a contact

If a cop shows enough interest in you to make contact, it's very likely he has a hunch that you're up to something. **You have only two goals at this stage:** First, not to give him anything more than he *believes* he already has, and second, to leave his presence. That's why it's best to separate from him right then, while *you* have the upper hand. *Nothing good* can come from you hanging around. Leave and get out of sight.

By *voluntarily* talking you might somehow give the cop grounds for detention or arrest—*even though you're completely innocent of any crime!* I can't emphasize this strongly enough. I fully realize that this goes against the peculiarly American grain of innocent openness, but you absolutely must learn when and how to *shut up!* You could, unwittingly, admit to having been at/near a crime scene, or knowing somebody criminally implicated. You could even "confess" to something you had no idea *was* a crime.

There is *no* advantage to answering questions about yourself during a contact. *Ever.* The *only* place to defend yourself is in a jury trial. Let the State drag you there *without your help.* **Offer/answer nothing—*ever!*** Even though he can *ask* you anything, you do *not* have to answer. You can simply ignore him, or reply something like:

> *"I don't have time to talk right now. Good day."*
> *"Sorry, but if I'm late again, it's my job!"*
> *"I can't believe you'd ask such a personal question!"*
> *"I was brought up not to talk to strangers."*

. . . and walk away, as from any airport Moonie. Almost any kind of departure will work here. Just keep it short and sweet.

If illegally carrying a weapon during a contact

You're at a severe disadvantage if on foot. In a car you have ample time and means to secure a weapon (as thoroughly explained in Chapter 4), but *not* as a pedestrian. So, be careful how/when you carry in public, *especially* in states which have no open or conceal carry provision. Cops are good at discerning concealed weapons—their lives *depend* on it. Pistol fanny packs are well known, at least in big cities. Shoulder holsters are fairly conspicuous. Inside the pants under a heavy shirt, vest, or jacket is best. Don't do so unless you are 100% discreet.

Avoid making contact with the police if you're carrying illegally (*i.e.*, a *malum prohibitum*). Don't make eye contact, but smoothly change directions and glide away. Should a contact be unavoidable, leaving is still your top priority, even if only to round a corner and ditch your weapon temporarily. The courts will justify almost *any* preemptive frisk for weapons as the cop's legal right, so you don't want to prolong a contact until he suddenly decides on a *Terry* frisk.

Stay calm and cool!

Overall, this is the important thing: *do not act nervous.* Nervousness, combined with other variables *might* be enough to create reasonable suspicion in the cop's mind. Do not keep looking back, do not run, do not begin rearranging your stuff, do not head directly for a phone. In other words, don't freak out. Just get away.

Personally, my exodus is not usually so abrupt as I often talk to him a bit to discover why he's sniffing about, *and* to keep up my edge. (I don't recommend such for the beginner, obviously. Stay squeaky-clean and you won't *need* an edge. With all my experience at this, even *I* don't needlessly stretch out a contact. This can be a high stakes dialogue, and you might have a really clever cop who wheedles something damaging from you.

When to increase your wariness

If the cop for some reason *does* become suspicious of you, it takes keen experience to sense the subtle shift. **"Friendly Cop" can slide into Suspicious Cop without missing a beat.** (The *eyes* are the giveaway; they'll become tighter and more focussed. This is why cops often wear sunglasses.) Be polite, but remain coolly wary. Cops work for the State, and the State is in search of *bodies.* When his eyes tighten and his questions become slightly more personal—*beware.*

The pedestrian advantage

Oh, one last thing. Most contacts are pedestrian, versus detentions/arrests on the road (where you've *already* been stopped for some infraction). I would *not*, therefore, return directly to your car, especially if the contact was rather eerie or inexplicable. A clever IC or RC can concoct a dozen pretexts to detain or even arrest you on the road ("speeding," "rolling through a stop sign," "failure to signal," etc.). Detention or arrest is much more difficult when you're just walking down the street. Indirectly return to your car without him seeing.

Once, I *did* experience a mere contact with police on the road. I had stopped to free a sticking choke and a highway patrolman pulled over behind me a minute later. I was lawfully wearing my pistol in plain view. Instead of letting *him* get out and initiate the Scene, I walked back, explained my problem through his window, thanked him for his concern, and returned to my car—not letting him say a *word!* He sat there, stunned, for about 20 seconds. I never looked back at him. He then drove away. Being polite and taking charge goes a long way.

Such is the best policy during any contact with police.

THE DETENTION

This not an arrest, but an *"intermediate level of intrusion"* which is a brief and so-called *"reasonable"* suspension of your freedom until the cop can uncover the required *"probable cause"* for arrest. As ruled in *Adams v. Williams,* 407 US 143 (1972):

> *The Fourth Amendment does not require a policeman who lacks the precise level of information for probable cause to simply shrug his shoulders and allow a crime to occur or a criminal to escape. On the contrary...it may be the essence of good police work to [detain the suspect].*

If you are lawfully detained, it's probably because you made yourself conspicuous and stupidly attracted attention.

Legal basis for detentions

According to *Terry v. Ohio* 392 US 1 (1968) a detention/stop *must* be based on *"reasonable articulable suspicion"* (RAS) that you were/are involved in some criminal activity. RAS is more than a mere hunch. It is the combination of several *facts* which a reasonable officer would conclude as articulable suspicion, such as:

❶ Concealment
❷ Flight at sight of officers
❸ Unusual movements
❹ Abandonment of property
❺ "Casing" a place
❻ Checking back and forth as a "look out" man would
❼ Disguises
❽ Presence at scene of a crime
❾ Information from a reliable informant

Usually, though not always, the courts require more than one of the above as a *pattern* of conduct. Merely being out late at night and briefly peering through a store window, by example, would probably not be enough to create RAS. Going *back* to the store and acting furtively probably *would* create RAS. Clearly, there are no hard rules here, so beware. Don't behave so suspiciously that *you'd* phone the police on somebody *else* doing what you're doing. Examples of a cop's experience-based information are:

❶ High crime area
❷ Suspect does not "fit" in neighborhood
❸ Suspect is a known addict, burglar, etc.
❹ Manner of packaging (especially drugs)
❺ Smells (*e.g.*, marijuana)
❻ Association with known criminals

Even *innocent* actions can add up to RAS
Under the totality of the circumstances test for investigatory stops, an officer may rely on combination of otherwise innocent observations to briefly pull over a suspect vehicle.

...It was a minivan, a type of automobile that Stoddard knew smugglers used. As it approached, it slowed dramatically, from about 50-55 to 25-30 miles per hour. He saw five occupants inside. An adult man was driving, an adult woman sat in the front passenger seat, and three children were in the back. The driver appeared stiff and his posture very rigid. He did not look at Stoddard and seemed to be trying to pretend that Stoddard was not there. Stoddard thought this suspicious because in his experience on patrol most persons look over and see what is going on, and in that area most drivers give border patrol agents a friendly wave.
— US v. Arvizu (2002)

Beware how the *totality* of your actions may appear to an officer. Do not decelerate dramatically, and do not rigidly drive by him. Most people at least glance at cops on the roadside, and so should you in general. (Waving, however, is up to you. Remember, too much of a "white flag" can be a red flag.)

The cop's powers during a *Terry* detention
These have, predictably, increased since my 1996 book. The *Terry* detention is the most legally gray scene (and inherently so, as it was created by the Court in 1968). Expect more police power expansion here over the next decade.

He may, with RAS or PC, use a traffic stop as a pretext

A unanimous 1996 case overturned the prohibition of pretextual stops. As long as the cop has RAS or PC on you, he can use any traffic violation to detain you for ulterior purposes.

The temporary detention of a motorist upon probable cause to believe that he has violated the traffic laws does not violate the Fourth Amendment's prohibition against unreasonable seizures, even if a reasonable officer would not have stopped the motorist absent some additional law enforcement objective.
— *Whren v. US*, 517 US 806 (1996)

He may order you and your passengers out of the car

According to *Pennsylvania v. Mimms* (1977) an officer may, for his safety, order the driver out of his car.

Maryland v. Wilson (1997) extended the *Mimms* rule to passengers. Justice Kennedy dissented in this 8-1 decision, opining that, *"Liberty comes not from officials by grace but from the Constitution by right."*

He may now (since June 2004) legally demand your name

Some states have so-called "stop and identify" laws whereby the cop may demand that you give your name during a lawful detention. (This is *not* the same thing as being required to show ID.) These laws were upheld in June 2004 by the Supreme Court ruling *Hiibel v. Sixth Judicial Court of Nevada*.

The scene: police responded to a domestic abuse call and found Lawrence Hiibel parked on the street. He refused 11 times to give his name. (Download the video from www.papersplease.org.) He was then arrested for violating Nevada statute §171.123(3), even though his identity was not in question due to witnesses.

In a 5-4 decision, the Court claimed that one's mere name is not inherently self-incriminatory, and thus not protected by the 5th. (Such assumes that the detainee is not wanted by police for another matter.) However, all the cop may legally demand is your name. Once you've stated or written it, you are not required to provide ID (unless a driver in a traffic stop).

As we understand it, the statute does not require a suspect to give the officer a driver's license or any other document. Provided that the suspect either states his name or communicates it to the officer by other means--a choice, we assume, that the suspect may make--the statute is satisfied and no violation occurs. See id., at ___, 59 P. 3d, at 1206-1207.

> *Further, the statutory obligation does not go beyond*
> *answering an officer's request to disclose a name.*
> — *Hiibel v. Sixth Judicial Court of Nevada*

You are *not* required to answer further questions, such as where you're going, what you do for a living, what's in your trunk, etc.

The four Justices' dissents are worth reading. Although I rarely agree with Stevens, Souter, Breyer, and Ginsberg, I do here:

> *Given a proper understanding of the category of "incriminating"*
> *communications that fall within the Fifth Amendment privilege* (sic), *it*
> *is clear that the disclosure of petitioner's identity is protected. The*
> *Court reasons that we should not assume that the disclosure of*
> *petitioner's name would be used to incriminate him or that it would*
> *furnish a link in a chain of evidence needed to prosecute him.* **But**
> **why else would an officer ask for it?** *And why else would the*
> *Nevada Legislature require its disclosure only when circumstances*
> *"reasonably indicate that the person has committed, is committing or*
> *is about to commit a crime"?* **If the Court is correct, then**
> **petitioner's refusal to cooperate did not impede the police**
> **investigation. Indeed, if we accept the predicate for the Court's**
> **holding, the statute requires nothing more than a useless**
> **invasion of privacy.** *I think that, on the contrary, the Nevada*
> *Legislature intended to provide its police officers with a useful law*
> *enforcement tool, and that the very existence of the statute*
> *demonstrates the value of the information it demands.*
> — Justice Stevens, dissenting

Stevens is right on: if your name cannot be incriminating, then why would the cop ask for it? And since Lawrence "Dudley" Hiibel was easily identified by others on scene, why arrest him for his silence?

> [The] *lengthy history--of concurring opinions, of references, and of*
> *clear explicit statements--means that the Court's statement in Berke-*
> *mer, while technically dicta, is the kind of strong dicta that the legal*
> *community typically takes as a statement of the law. And that law*
> *has remained undisturbed for more than 20 years.*
>   **There is no good reason now to reject this generation-old**
> **statement of the law.** *There are sound reasons rooted in Fifth*
> *Amendment considerations for adhering to this Fourth Amendment*
> *legal condition circumscribing police authority to stop an individual*
> *against his will. See ante, at 1-6 (Stevens, J., dissenting). Adminis-*
> *trative considerations also militate against change. Can a State, in*
> *addition to requiring a stopped individual to answer "What's your*
> *name?" also require an answer to "What's your license number?" or*
> *"Where do you live?" Can a police officer, who must know how to*
> *make a Terry stop, keep track of the constitutional answers?* **After**

all, answers to any of these questions may, or may not, incriminate, depending upon the circumstances.
— Justice Breyer, with whom Justice Souter and Justice Ginsburg join, dissenting

Hiibel affirms merely the police power to demand your name in a *Terry* stop—not produce your driver's license, passport, etc. (much less compel one to answer further questions). Look into the "stop and identify" statute of your own state. As a result of *Hiibel*, at most you can be required to state or write your name, but that is *not* the same thing as actually producing identification documents (even though the newspapers' shoddy coverage of *Hiibel* often states this erroneous interpretation).

While "stop and identify" laws remain unconstitutional during a mere suspicionless contact encounter (*Brown v. Texas*, 443 US 47 (1979)), you sadly no longer have the previously perfect 5th Amendment right of silence during a lawful detention.

"What's the big deal?" you may ask. OK, how about this: the cops ask your name and you give it. They run a computer check and find an outstanding traffic ticket. Or, they see your name in the gun owner database (compiled by many states) or the concealed-carry permit database—and thus subject you to an immediate *Terry* frisk of your person and car interior. If a firearm is found that (unbeknownst to you) has a stolen past or was prohibited *ex post facto* (such as the USAS-12 and Street Sweeper 12ga shotguns), then having simply given your name will result in your arrest. Nifty.

Although *Hiibel* does not allow a systemwide ID check, it does help pave the way for such in the future. We are just a few laws away from biometric "Homeland Security" National ID Cards, gun registration, and owner licensing. Stay tuned.

He may ask you questions (but you don't have to answer)

[The] *officer may ask the [Terry] detainee a moderate number of questions to...try to obtain information confirming or dispelling the officer's suspicions. But the detainee is not obliged to respond.*
— *Berkemer v. McCarty*, 468 US 420, 439 (1984)

The Court's original (and abiding) rationale in 1968 *Terry* was that since detainees have to suffer the new intermediate level of seizure, they are not required to answer questions (beyond their name, according to 2004 *Hiibel*).

He may physically restrain you, if necessary

If you do not stop, or attempt to leave, the cop may restrain you in a manner reasonable when considered in light of the purpose. If you try to flee or struggle, the cop may even cuff you, especially if you are suspected of a violent crime. However, if the cop handcuffs a compliant detainee in a non-emergency, the *"seizure" will* be considered an unlawful arrest by the court.

He does not have to "read you your rights"

No *"Miranda"* warning is required prior actual custodial arrest, so *you* must be aware of your rights because the cop will not inform you until *after* an arrest. (More on this in Chapter 9.)

He does not have to inform you of your right of refusal

This was reaffirmed in the 2002 *US v. Drayton* in which two bus passengers consented to a search of their person and then later claimed that the alleged contact was in reality a detention (due to the three officers having basically commandeered a sitting bus, whose driver had left) without reasonable suspicion:

> *The Court has rejected in specific terms the suggestion that police officers must always inform citizens of their right to refuse when seeking permission to conduct a warrantless consent search. See, e.g., Ohio v. Robinette, 519 U. S. 33, 39-40 (1996); Schneckloth v. Bustamonte, 412 U. S. 218, 227 (1973). "While knowledge of the right to refuse consent is one factor to be taken into account, the government need not establish such knowledge as the sine qua non of an effective consent."*

This was an interesting detention case, and one difficult to decide. It's worth reading *US v. Drayton*, especially Souter's dissent:

> *...The reasonable inference was that the "interdiction" was not a consensual exercise, but one the police would carry out whatever the circumstances; that they would prefer "cooperation" but would not let the lack of it stand in their way. There was no contrary indication that day, since no passenger had refused the cooperation requested, and there was no reason for any passenger to believe that the driver would return and the trip resume until the police were satisfied. The scene was set and an atmosphere of obligatory participation was established by this introduction. Later requests to search prefaced with "Do you mind ..." would naturally have been understood in the terms with which the encounter began.*
> *...The situation is much like the one in the alley, with civilians in close quarters, unable to move effectively, being told their cooperation is expected. While I am not prepared to say that no bus*

> *interrogation and search can pass the Bostick test without a warning that passengers are free to say no, the facts here surely required more from the officers than a quiet tone of voice. A police officer who is certain to get his way has no need to shout.*

Such faintly menacing contacts are pretty common:

> *Drug Enforcement Administration officers will board an Amtrak train, crowd into the doorway of someone's private roomette and bother them with a long serious of questions about where they're going without giving them Miranda warnings. It's all premised on the no-tion that the suspect is free to leave and that the encounter is con-sensual. But that premise is a myth.*
> — Albuquerque attorney Pete Schoenburg
> 29 March 1998 *Seattle Times*, p.A16

You may be *Terry* frisked for weapons

But only if the cop has a good faith belief that you might be armed *and he has a particular fear of his safety.* Realistically, he will frisk pretty routinely, so beware.

He may bring eyewitnesses to the scene to confront you

He may conduct a limited investigation of crimes (*e.g.*, to determine if the detainee can be identified as a suspect).

He may hold a detainee for at least 20-30 minutes

The cop generally has this long to find *"probable cause"* for an arrest, or you're free to go. While the courts have not and cannot set a rigid time limit, 90 minutes is *usually* too long, 60 minutes *probably* is, and 45 minutes is a legal coin toss.

What is *"reasonable"* depends on the circumstances, the officer's degree of diligence and his use of the least intrusive means to confirm his suspicions. He cannot drag his feet trying to buy time. Anything beyond 30 minutes will certainly require a good explanation, proof of diligence and the least intrusion.

If, however, you've landed at an international airport and the feds have RAS that you're a "swallower" (somebody who smuggles heroin or cocaine in swallowed condoms), all rationality goes out the window. In *U.S. v. Odofin,* 929 F.2d 56 (2nd Cir. 1991), a Nigerian landed at JFK and was detained as a swallower. He refused to sub-mit to an X-ray or intake laxatives, so the feds held him until he passed his stomach contents. Normally this happens within 24-48 hours, but Odofin was committed to waiting them out. He did so for *24 days . . .* and his detention was *upheld!* The court "reasoned" that

Odofin himself was responsible for the length of his detention since he didn't submit to radiation or laxatives. Groan.

Your rights during a detention

For you, my law-abiding, informed reader, I'd say it's about 70/30, favoring you. (For the ignorant sap—usually a criminal—it drops to 10/90.)

Without RAS or PC you *can't* be stopped for a DL check

*2. **Except where** there is at least articulable and reasonable suspicion that a motorist is unlicensed or that an automobile is not registered, or that either the vehicle or an occupant is otherwise subject to seizure for violation of law, **stopping an automobile and detaining the driver in order to check his driver's license and the registration of the automobile are unreasonable under the Fourth Amendment**. Pp. 653-663.*

(a) Stopping an automobile and detaining its occupants constitute a "seizure" within the meaning of the Fourth and Fourteenth Amendments, even though the purpose of the stop is limited and the resulting detention quite brief. The permissibility of a particular law enforcement practice is judged by balancing its intrusion on the individual's Fourth Amendment interests against its promotion of legitimate governmental interests. Pp. 653-655. [440 U.S. 648, 649]

(b) The State's interest in discretionary spot checks as a means of ensuring the safety of its roadways does not outweigh the resulting intrusion on the privacy and security of the persons detained. Given the physical and psychological intrusion visited upon the occupants of a vehicle by a random stop to check documents, cf. United States v. Brignoni-Ponce, 422 U.S. 873; United States v. Martinez-Fuerte, 428 U.S. 543, the marginal contribution to roadway safety possibly resulting from a system of spot checks cannot justify subjecting every occupant of every vehicle on the roads to a seizure at the unbridled discretion of law enforcement officials. Pp. 655-661.

(c) An individual operating or traveling in an automobile does not lose all reasonable expectation of privacy simply because the automobile and its use are subject to government regulation. People are not shorn of all Fourth Amendment protection when they step from their homes onto the public sidewalk; nor are they shorn of those interests when they step from the sidewalks into their automobiles. Pp. 662-663.

(d) The holding in this case does not preclude Delaware or other States from developing methods for spot checks that involve less

intrusion or that do not involve the unconstrained exercise of discretion. **Questioning of all oncoming traffic at roadblock-type stops is one possible alternative.** *Pp. 663.*
— *Delaware v. Prouse,* 440 US 648 (1979)

To my knowledge, no case testing the veiled recommendation of universal roadblock questioning has yet come before the Court. No doubt, however, that many departments are experiementing with the *"questioning of all incoming traffic"* at roadblocks.

You may *not* be forcibly moved to a police car or station

Though you are *not* free to walk away, being unnecessarily placed in custody constitutes an unlawful arrest without PC.

Outside a traffic stop, you *don't* have to show your DL

The legal rationale for the intermediate level of intrusion of the detention is that *answers are consensual.* State your name (as now required), but do not provide any ID papers or DL.

You do *not* have to answer questions beyond your name

Though you do *not* have to answer questions, failure to do so will tend to raise, not dispel, the cop's suspicions. He may then be justified in giving you a *Terry* frisk. All this means is that the detention will last a bit longer. Big deal. He won't like your reticence. Big deal. Your goal is to avoid being arrested, and if silence is the surest route, then so be it. What he's looking for is probable cause, or something which *leads* to PC.

If PC doesn't exist, then you're *free* after a few minutes

Unless he *concocts* PC, which *is* a possibility. Even if PC *does* exist, you're free if he can't find it before the clock runs out. Time is on *your* side. Also, to my understanding, you have the right to demand that he express his RAS to you.

Try to leave (*i.e.,* assert your rights, don't assume!)

If the cop won't articulate his *"reasonable suspicion"* upon demand, say, *"Since you have expressed no legal basis for any detention, then I must be free to go"* and then attempt to leave. You call his bluff, or force him to detain you (lawfully or unlawfully).

The roadblock detention

You are likely to encounter a *"brief, suspicionless seizure at a fixed checkpoint"* at least once a year. So far, they are restricted in scope to intercepting illegal aliens and drunks. They cannot be too generalized in purpose, else they offend the 4th Amendment.

The principal protection of Fourth Amendment rights at checkpoints lies in appropriate limitations on the scope of the stop.
— *U.S. v. Martinez-Fuerte*, 428 US 543, 566-567 (1976)

[Roadblock seizures are consistent with the Fourth Amendment if they are] *carried out pursuant to a plan embodying explicit, neutral limitations on the conduct of individual officers.*
[Specifically, the constitutionality of a seizure turns upon] *a weighing of the gravity of the public concerns served by the seizure, the degree to which the seizure advances the public interest, and the severity of the interference with individual liberty.*
— *Brown v. Texas*, 443 US 47, 50-51 (1979)

Roadblocks cannot be too generalized in purpose

Held: Because the [drug] *checkpoint program's primary purpose is indistinguishable from the general interest in crime control, the checkpoints violate the Fourth Amendment.*

*(a) **The rule that a search or seizure is unreasonable under the Fourth Amendment absent individualized suspicion of wrongdoing has limited exceptions.** For example, this Court has upheld brief, suspicionless seizures at a fixed checkpoint designed to intercept illegal aliens, United States v. Martinez-Fuerte, 428 U. S. 543, and at a sobriety checkpoint aimed at removing drunk drivers from the road, Michigan Dept. of State Police v. Sitz, 496 U.S. 444. The Court has also suggested that a similar roadblock to verify drivers' licenses and registrations would be permissible to serve a highway safety interest. Delaware v. Prouse, 440 U. S. 648, 663. **However, the Court has never approved a checkpoint program whose primary purpose was to detect evidence of ordinary criminal wrongdoing.** Pp. 3-7.*
— *City of Indianapolis v. Edmond* (2000)

A police checkpoint finally too generalized for the Court! Amazing! Rhenquist and Scalia, however, whined about the ruling:

The reasonableness of highway checkpoints, at issue here, turns on whether they effectively serve a significant state interest with minimal intrusion on motorists.

Well, gee, what couldn't be construed as a *"significant state interest with minimal intrusion on motorists"*? Justice Thomas saw the danger of this in his intriguing dissent:

> Taken together, our decisions in Michigan Dept. of State Police v. Sitz, 496 U. S. 444 (1990), and United States v. Martinez-Fuerte, 428 U. S. 543 (1976), stand for the proposition that suspicionless roadblock seizures are constitutionally permissible if conducted according to a plan that limits the discretion of the officers conducting the stops. **I am not convinced that Sitz and Martinez-Fuerte were correctly decided.** Indeed, I rather doubt that the Framers of the Fourth Amendment would have considered "reasonable" a program of indiscriminate stops of individuals not suspected of wrongdoing.
>
> — Justice Thomas, dissenting

Clarence Thomas has toyed with strict constructionalism for years, but can't ever *quite* seem to go there. While I think he's clearly brilliant, he really is too much of a *tease* to be useful. He occasionally shows us some libertarian thigh, but never undresses for bed.

The cop's powers during a roadblock detention

Since these seizures are conducted *without* particularized suspicion on the motorists, cops would not seem to have **Hiibel** authority to demand your name. They can pull you over and ask you questions and circle a drug dog around your car, but they cannot (without RAS or PC) demand your name or that you exit your car.

Your rights during a roadblock detention

Not quite as many as during a contact, *but almost* since the seizure is without RAS. **Refuse to answer any questions, and refuse to consent to any searches.** Unless they've some plain view PC on you, there's really nothing they can do to a properly noncooperative roadblock detainee beyond a brief delay.

Visit www.roadblock.org for more tips and info.

The ag diesel roadblock detention

In Arizona the cops were stopping highway drivers of diesel trucks and SUVs to discover if they were using tax-free agricultural fuel in violation of law. A reader friend of mine got dragooned into this, and complained so effectively to the Arizona AG's office that they shut them down the next day. Go and do likewise!

What's my risk of being detained?

Assuming you've prepared yourself as described, the chances of a detention are slim. As I mentioned in Chapter 4, cops *rarely* roust a clean-cut, law-abiding type. Also, they show remarkable restraint in rousting the scruffier types. On the whole, whenever *I've* been detained, the cops usually had a valid reason by legal standards. In my dozens of detentions, I was legitimately stopped about 90% of the time (usually for "speeding," etc.). Only about 10% was I ever originally stopped for basically no reason or, worse yet, some truly concocted pretext.

So, if you're detained, the odds are that you've done something to give the cop RAS (*e.g.*, a "traffic" offense, or that you're unlawfully concealing a weapon). The *next* most likely reason is that by innocently being at the wrong place at the wrong time, you've unawaredly immersed yourself in an investigation. (The family dog *can* be caught in a wolf trap.) This has happened to me several times, and I didn't understand why until they had asked a few illuminating questions. Finally, the *least* likely scenario is that you're simply being rousted *without* legal cause.

So, if you don't give the cops cause for attention, the only way to be detained is by unaware proximity/association with a crime, or textbook rousting. Either are pretty rare.

Practical tips during a detention

A mere contact can easily and subtly ripen into a detention. If you feel increasingly not at liberty to leave, the situation has probably sunk to a detention. Although cops are allegedly instructed to reassure the contact of his freedom to go, as well as announce when the situation has ripened into a detention, they are *rarely* this candid. Once, when an RC was rousting me for my lawfully holstered pistol, I had to inquire *three* times if I was being detained! When he realized that his bullying tactics did not make me wet my pants, he retreated, gave me his little lecture and stomped off.

There is a simple way to clarify the Scene—**you should express a *firm, clear* desire to leave and ask him if you are free to go.** Don't respond to questions or demands *until* he's answered this. If you are being detained, he *must* admit it. Be polite, but firm, and keep him in his place. *He's* bound by more case law and procedure than you—never let him forget it.

Handling an obvious fishing expedition

The best reply to random snoopy questions is, *"I don't have to answer that."* It's true, it's elegantly simple, and it's effective. For the most part, it is all you need to know.

My defense attorney friend Marc Victor in Phoenix mentioned a related tip. If you reply, *"My attorney told me not to answer such questions"* the cop cannot even later repeat your answer because of attorney/client confidentiality. www.lawyersforfreedom.com

Handling the Scene when the cop has RAS

The cop's questions *must* relate to the purpose of the stop (his RAS), or else the detention is unreasonable. That's why you should *first* pry from him his RAS so that you can keep his questioning within proper bounds.

Cop: *"No, you are not free to go, and yes, I'm detaining you. You've walked up and down this block three times in the past half hour, looking around like you're casing the area. I've never seen you before around here, and your actions are suspicious to me."*
You: *"Oh, I see! A friend told me to meet her at a store to help pick out a gift, but I forgot the name. I was hoping to run into her or maybe remember the store by walking around, and was about to call her when you came up to me."*

Your response is perfectly believable and should at once allay his suspicion. A reasonable explanation *should* spring you. Some cops, however, will probe a bit further:

Cop: *"How were you planning to call her if she's at some store you don't even know the name of?"*
You: *"Well, fortunately she carries her cell phone in her purse."*

At this point, by the cop's probe of your story, you should be *quite* on guard. I would quickly and smoothly change the tenor of the situation by offering, *"Hey, I can call her from this pay phone to find out where she's at and then you can tell me how to get to the store. I'd really appreciate that! She's probably wondering by now what happened to me."* By taking charge you've changed the dynamics and totally deflated the Scene. First, you proved your story was true and then "demoted" him into a mere directions-giver. There's little way he could refuse.

If innocently caught up in another's crime

Let's say you're out jogging late at night. A house is hit a few streets over by a burglar in a dark running suit, though you're unaware of this. A cop spots you, has RAS because your proximity and resemblance to the burglar, and detains you. Any reasonable person would conclude that he is not free to go, and that state of mind is the legal basis for determining detention vs. mere contact.

You must be *very* careful here. Even though you are utterly innocent of the burglary, there is a significant chance that you might be arrested and even convicted.

Cop: (Polite, though firm:) *"Evening, Sir. May I see some ID?"*
You: (Polite, though not slavish:) *"Good evening, Officer. What's this all about? Are you detaining or arresting me?"*
Cop: (Less polite:) *"No, Sir, you're not under arrest, but I am detaining you as a possible suspect in a local matter. Do you have some ID?"*
You: (Absolutely calm:) *"My name is _____. I'd like to get back to my jogging now. I am I free to go?"*

You have complied with the "stop and identify" statute of your state (assuming it has one). You are not required to answer any further questions! You've asked him his reason for stopping you—his RAS. You've expressed your desire to go.

The ball is now in his court. If he replies in an appeased tone that there was a burglary on Pine Street and he was checking out anybody matching the burglar's description, then you're probably home free. However, if he seems to be "having none of it" and persists in a suspicious tone, beware:

Cop: (Not satisfied:) *"Were you on Pine Street a few minutes ago?"*

Your alarm bells should *really* be going off now! He is still fairly convinced that you're the burglar. Your goal at this crucial point is to stand firm and not give the cop *anything* to allow an extended detention or a possible arrest.

If you *do* admit to having been on Pine, he will then have cause to detain you further until the homeowner is brought to identify you. If you are unlucky enough to have the same general height, build and appearance of the burglar—and the conditions were poor enough—there's a good chance of being erroneously fingered.

You: (Reasonable:) *"Look, I haven't done anything wrong. Did something just happen over on Pine Street?"*
Cop: (Intense:) *"Just answer me—were you on Pine tonight?"*

You: (Polite, though a bit more firm:) *"Now, Officer, this is concerning me. I mean, put yourself in my shoes. You're out jogging, minding your own business, get suddenly pulled over and asked your whereabouts earlier. I haven't done anything wrong, and I don't know of any crimes just committed on Pine—or else I would have already phoned in. Now, I think I have a right to know what's going on here, don't you?"*

By *not* jumping into any legal arguments/demands and retaining a common-sense "I-haven't-done-anything-wrong" position, you have kept the Scene mature and reasonable. The cop should realize that you're just an innocent jogger, soften up and explain. However, if you've got an IC or RC, it gets tougher:

Cop: (Now angry:) *"No, you don't 'have the right to know what's going on here'! You need to start answering my questions! Were you on Pine Street a few minutes ago?"*

If you *were* on Pine Street—do *not* lie. I understand it would be tempting to deny it and get the cop out of your face, but it can easily come back to bite you later. For example, it's possible that somebody either saw you there or can say that you regularly jog on Pine—and either will impeach the *rest* of your story, which is truthful. To succeed through lying requires: ❶ the cop to *believe* it, and ❷ *nobody* (including *yourself* through stupidity or forgetfulness) disputing it later. These are *not* reliable odds.

Besides, since you are *not compelled* to answer, there's no reason to lie to an officer, which is a crime (even if not under oath). According to 18 USC §3C1.1 you can receive a *"sentence enhancement"* for (among other things) *"making false statements, not under oath, to law enforcement officers"* and *"providing incomplete or misleading information, not amounting to a material falsehood, in respect to a pre-sentence investigation."*

Yet, cops can lie to us, in and out of court, with impunity. On 20 December 2000, US Solicitor General Seth P. Waxman defended to the 9th Circuit Court FBI sniper Lon Horiuchi in the attempted Idaho prosecution for manslaughter of Vicky Weaver:

> *These federal law enforcement officials are privileged to do what would otherwise be unlawful if done by a private citizen.* ***It's a fundamental function of our government.***
>
> [To prosecute Horiuchi] *would cast a chill on discretionary judgments officers have to make.* (BTP: That was rather the point!)

Committing unlawful acts is *"a fundamental function of our government"*? Stunned, Judge Alex Kozinski inquired, *"If the Constitution does not provide limitations for federal agents' actions, then what does?"* Indeed.

So, do not lie to cops. You might handle it something like this:

You: (Not rising to his anger, though quite firm:)   *"Officer, I don't want this to get out of hand here. I understand that you're trying to do your job and apparently something just happened on Pine. Whatever it was I had no part in and whoever did is getting away right now. I'm trying to help you here, but know nothing about any crimes committed. This is all I have to say and I'd like to be on my way right now. Am I free to go?"*

The above volunteers nothing even indirectly damaging, restates with firmness your innocence and forces the cop to decide whether he can detain you further. The most he can do is bring the homeowner over to identify you.

As I said, this is a *highly* dangerous predicament. I would protest such as extremely prejudicial against you as the recently burglarized homeowner is likely to be quite emotional and intent on finding the thief. This state of mind, and the unavoidably incriminating fact that the cop *already* has you detained as a suspect, clearly *begs* for a classic misidentification. I would further insist that a formal lineup is the only way to be fair, especially since there's no evidence of your being on Pine.

If he remains intent on a solitary field check by the homeowner, I would raise a good stink and demand that your attorney be notified first. A few years of your life are at stake here.

Handling yourself during a roust

Cop: (Matter-of-fact:)   *"What's in your bag?"*
You: (Breezy:)   *"Lawful private property. I'm surprised you'd ask such a personal question! Sorry, but I've things to do—am I free to go?*
Cop: (Mildly sarcastic:)   *"Well, if it's 'lawful private property' then there's no reason to mind if I had a look, is there?"*
You: (Coolly indignant:)   *"As a matter of fact, I would mind. It's a waste of my time as a law-abiding Citizen and a waste of your time as a peace officer in search of criminals. As I said, I've got a rather busy day and must be on my way. Am I free to go, or are you detaining me?*
Cop: (Stern:)   *"You mean you won't let me look in your bag?"*
You: (Firm:)   *"That's right. I wish to leave now—am I free to go?"*
Cop: *"No, you are not free to go. I'm detaining you."*

You: (Casually pulling out your digital voice recorder, pushing "record" and holding the microphone up:) *"Oh, you're detaining me? Is this based on reasonable articulable suspicion?"*

Cop: (Clearly surprised at and a bit unrattled by your cool preparedness and thorough knowledge of procedure:) *"Of course it is."*

You: *"Oh, and what is your reasonable suspicion?"*

Cop: (A little hot:) *"How do you know about that?"*

You: (Cool:) *"Well, I'm studied in the law, but not yet admitted in this state.* (This is a great line to use, which he will naturally infer to mean that you are an attorney.) *I'm beginning to wonder if you indeed have any legal basis for stopping me. I'm asking you again to please articulate, for the legal record, your 'reasonable suspicion' for detaining me."*

Cop: (A bit flustered:) *"Your refusing to allow a search of your bag."*

You: (Cool but firm:) *"You need to catch up on the law, Officer. My refusal in no way gives you 'reasonable suspicion'—as U.S. v. Manuel ruled back in 1993. If you detain me based on that, then you're personally liable for an unlawful restraint. Now, unless you have some actual RAS, I'd like to go now."*

At this point, you've boxed him into a corner, and the cop must either: ❶ Let you go realizing that his bluff has failed and that pushing it will likely get him in trouble, or ❷ Articulate some true *"reasonable suspicion"* to support a lawful detention.

If he turns you loose, snort disgustingly and *leave.* While a smart parting line may seem irresistible, *don't.* You've already won, he *knows* it, and you must settle for that. Later, if you want to write a brief letter complaining that he held you up because of his ignorance of the law, that's up to you. But then and there, just *leave.*

However, let's suppose that he *does* state some kind of valid RAS. If so, then he's got a lawful detention. Do not try to leave. Do not bluster or get upset. The situation (assuming you're behaving lawfully) is *still* in your favor 70/30. Stay calm, but increase your wariness. (A perfect example of this was portrayed by Paul Scofield as Sir Thomas More when interrogated by Cromwell in the 1966 Best Picture *A Man For All Seasons.* Cool and sharp.)

The roust continues; what about concocted RAS?

How easy a thing it is to find a staff if a man be minded to beat a dog.

—Thomas Becon, *Early Works: Preface* (1563)

Most RCs and many ICs *will* fudge on RAS if they feel that you're dirty and PC is likely, or if you've made a real nuisance of yourself.

Basically, the first thing you really learn as a cop is how to lie. Now, say you see some guy driving who you think is wrong. **You stop him on no basis that could stand up in court.** *So you lie if you* **have to.** *You say he ran a STOP sign or didn't signal or had a broken taillight that you break after you've determined he's bad. That makes the initial stop legal.*

[Then] *you search the car, which you generally have no probable cause to do.* [If contraband is found then] *lie and testify that the guy gave you permission to search... Sure, you've fabricated the probable cause and done an illegal search, but the guy is bad, right?* **We do what we have to do.**

— a convicted Philadelphia police officer, "How Cops Go Bad," *TIME*, 15 Dec 1997

If there are no friendly witnesses around, beware. The old *"I detected the smell of marijuana"* is practically unbeatable, for example. (If this ever happened to me, I'd try to *immediately* dragoon some countering noses from the passersby. Put such a cop on the defensive in front of witnesses before he "finds" something.)

Whatever the bogus RAS, I'd try to rope in some friendly witnesses, *immediately.* Done quickly enough, before an actual arrest, the cop should realize that his sham will dissolve under judicial scrutiny. You must be very bold here. Cause a mild ruckus, proclaiming that you are being framed or set up. You likely have little to lose with such a tactic.

What if they try to move me during a detention?

Although you're *not* to be moved around during detention, cops often do this (which elevates matters into an arrest).

Story in point: I know of somebody involved in a car accident who was later visited at work by the cops for routine questioning (mere contact). He was at his desk, carrying his pistol concealed in a gun fanny pack (which is lawful on one's own premises or at work). In what was probably a ruse, the cops asked him to follow them outside where they could "speak more freely." Once outside and in public, they (apparently knowing he was armed and having lured him into a trap) frisked him, confiscated his weapon and arrested him.

The only defense he has, in my opinion, is to assert that he was falsely "taken in custody" (arrested) when moved outside (because he thought he had no right to refuse), because the cops had no RAS to detain, much less PC to arrest.

His pistol, however, is probably gone even if he gets a favorable ruling. These days once your gun is confiscated, even unlawfully, you have about zero chance of seeing it again. If you conceal often without a permit, at least carry something less stinging to lose, like a Russian Makarov for $140 or an inexpensive .38 Special. It's silly to risk losing a tuned-up Colt Officer's Model, etc. Don't, however, sacrifice *too* much quality or caliber.

In retrospect, what he *should* have done was either refuse to leave his desk, or join them outside *after* he had discreetly left his pack behind. As I mentioned, it's always better to learn from the mistakes of *others*. **Don't *ever* allow a cop to trick or intimidate you into a worsened situation.** Occupy the highest ground possible (preferably contact) and *stay* there while you effect an exit.

Some final thoughts on detentions

If you're detained it means that you *blew* it, at least in some small way. Either you blew the contact when you *could* have simply walked away, or he detained you right off the bat (bypassing contact) because of your behavior. **You *blew* it.** Detention is the last step before arrest. Use wisdom and coolheadedness, and my Chapters 9-10 will be moot material.

A really shrewd cop will sometimes hold off on arresting (and therefore waiting to give the required *Miranda* warning) even though he's *already* got PC to arrest. He'll briefly postpone arrest in order to obtain more evidence from a talkative detainee (who usually doesn't know that he has the right *not* to answer questions). Once the suspect is actually arrested and *Mirandized*, the cop's chance of wheedling anything more is much reduced.

I mention this because *you* might sometime be detained when the cop already has PC to arrest. There's no way to reliably discern this, however. One solid clue is an overly confident, almost smug, attitude on his part. If the detaining cop seems unusually sure of himself and his questioning, he is likely to already have PC on you. I would then definitely answer his questions with, *"I have no knowledge of any crimes. I'd like to be on my way. Am I free to go?"* Run down the 20-30 minute clock of *"reasonableness"* with polite noncooperation and force him to either arrest or spring you.

A bit of *non-personalized* anger is often helpful here. The exact attitude to have is difficult to describe. Do not be snotty or sarcastic. Do not drop names or threaten a lawsuit. Do not stammer or avert your eyes. Do not clench your jaw, or cross your arms.

I'm trying to describe *anger without defiance*. The cop is used to wimps and hotheads. By not being either you will confuse him, and thereby create Doubt in his mind. By being gauntly cordial, and firm without fear, he will become unsure of himself, of the detention and of its consequences. If you do your part right, he *will* let you go.

It works. I've done it. So can you.

SEARCH & SEIZURE

The right of the people to be secure in their persons, houses, papers, and effects, against unreasonable searches and seizures, shall not be violated, and no warrants shall issue, but upon probable cause, supported by oath or affirmation, and particularly describing the place to be searched, and the persons or things to be seized.
— 4th Amendment to the Constitution

The modern Court has discovered that the purpose of the Fourth Amendment is to protect people's "reasonable expectations of privacy" and so this has become the Court's standard for determining how far law enforcement can go in conducting searches and seizures....

Now, because people's expectations of privacy vary in different circumstances, the Court has concluded that our Fourth Amendment rights similarly vary. So, case law now proclaims your rights are stronger in your home than when you are in your car. They are better if you own than if you rent. They are better if you build a solid privacy fence around your yard than if you put up a chain link fence. Your rights are stronger if you are a passenger in a car than if you are the driver. (BTP Note: This is increasingly less the case since 2001, as I'll explain.) Personal papers like letters and diaries are more protected than business records, etc. A different Fourth Amendment rule for every occasion!
— Jeff Snyder, *Nation of Cowards* (2001), p.141

Most people believe that all searches by the police require a warrant. Ah, if only that were true. Although PC is thankfully still prerequisite, the courts have carved out many exceptions to the warrant requirement. For example, there are "searches" which are not technically searches, and there are even searches which are deemed *not* to require a warrant. Alas, the residue (searches requiring a warrant) is quite meager.

"SEARCHES" WHICH AREN'T REALLY SEARCHES

The 4th Amendment does not protect against searches of places and objects which anyone may see. A "search" within constitutional contemplation means a police breach of private property. Beginning with *Katz v.US*, 389 US 347 the Court has carved out several exceptions which are not considered true searches under the 4th Amendment:

Abandoned Property

When the owner forfeits his proprietary interest in something by leaving it in a public place, such is deemed to be discarded (as garbage thrown in a public trash can) or abandoned (as a junker car left on the road). The police may seize such abandoned property without a warrant or even PC.

Open Fields

You're gonna love this: cops may trespass onto your land and observe you from the undeveloped or unoccupied portion of your property which lies outside the *"curtilage of a dwelling."* What on earth does *"curtilage"* mean? The area around the home to which your home life extends.

What lies in/outside your own curtilage is solely within local judicial interpretation and your property's characteristics.

There are no hard and fast rules—only guidelines. *Rosencranz v. U.S.*, 356 F2d 310, 313 (1st Cir. 1966) and *Wattenburg v. U.S.*, 388 F2d 853, 857-8 (9th Cir. 1968) spelled out the:

Factors which tend to embrace a structure within the curtilage include:
1) proximity or annexation to the house,
2) structures suggesting propinquity and absence of barriers (such as a driveway between the house and building),
3) inclusion within the general enclosure surrounding the house,
4) habitual use for family purposes, and
5) indications that...owner sought to protect a privacy interest.
— E.X. Boozhie, *The Outlaw's Bible*; p. 127

An open area fenced in and posted with "No Trespassing" signs can be an "open field" outside the curtilage. While such entry may indeed be criminal trespass, it does not offend the 4th Amendment (which protects merely *privacy,* not possessory, interests). The police may trespass and snoop around your land just because it's not used as much as your porch or backyard. (Ah, it's nice to live in such a "free" country! America is merely the healthiest patient in the cancer ward, that's all.)

"Plain View"

The police may, without a warrant, seize any contraband or evidence of a crime that is in *"plain view"* **and to which he has lawful access.** If you invite a cop inside your home or business, you've given him the legal right to be there and anything seen in plain view can be seized. In public places and in your car, you have a *"lessened expectation of privacy"* and are much more vulnerable to plain view/hearing/smell seizures.

The only prerequisite is that the cop *must* have PC that the item to be seized is indeed contraband or evidence.

Aerial Surveillance

Well, let's say the cops want to look in your backyard, but can't because it lies within the curtilage. The solution is up, up and away. Cops can fly over your backyard and it's not a "search." If what they see gives them PC, they will easily obtain a search warrant.

What's more, minimum altitude requirements don't affect the constitutionality of the flyover any more than does trespassing onto open fields. Conceivably, a helicopter could hover 100 feet over your home, snapping photos with a telephoto lens of your interior activities. (By the way, did I mention how nice it is to live in a "free" country?)

"sense-enhancing technology"

The 2001 ***Kyllo v. US*** ruled that the use of a thermal imaging device constituted an unreasonable search:

> *The government's use of a device that is not in general public use, to explore details of a private home that would previously have been unknowable without physical intrusion, is a Fourth Amendment "search" and presumptively unreasonable without a warrant.*

The obvious implication here is that once a formerly advanced piece of equipment is in general use and its capabilities known, your right of reasonable expectation of privacy is then lost.

What would be considered as in current general use? Parabolic mikes, radio scanners, and night vision devices, most assuredly. Beware. Once thermal imagers are sold by mail-order, they will no longer be prohibited in warrantless searches.

Controlled Deliveries

If the police have lawfully opened a container and identified its contents as contraband, they do not need a warrant to reopen it after a *"controlled delivery."* For example, if the postal workers "accidentally" discover (wink, wink) contraband mailed to you, the cops can reseal it, pose as your mailman for delivery, and arrest you.

If the cops *really* want somebody badly enough, they'll mail contraband to the mark and bust him. It appears that exactly this was done to federally licensed firearms dealer Al Woodbridge of Washington state. Incensed that Mr. Woodbridge was active in supporting the 2nd Amendment, machine gun parts were sent to him. When he signed for the unordered package (the contents of which were unknown to him), the BATF raided his shop. In an outrageous travesty of justice, he was convicted and is now serving time. **An indirect lesson here is: do *not* sign for unknown packages.** At least one fingerless victim of the Unabomber has learned this.

Private Searches

Only government officials are bound by the 4th Amendment. If a private Citizen discovers contraband within your property and tells the cops, they can follow up on the guy's intrusion with their own inspection. As long as the cops took no part in or encouraged the intrusion, they can use the information against you. *Beware* of whom you allow access to your property, such as guests, tenants, repairmen, salespeople, etc.

Impound and Post-arrest Inventories

Pursuant to departmental caretaking policy, a cop may conduct a warrantless inventory search of the passenger area, including glove box, of any lawfully impounded car. He may also open any closed containers for inventory purposes.

The same applies at the police station to the personal property (including closed containers) of an arrestee who is going to be booked and jailed. Heed Chapters 3 and 4!

SEARCHES WITHOUT A WARRANT

Now we arrive at true searches which *are* indeed within contemplation of the Constitution, but do *not* require a warrant. Many situations furnish the police with the PC necessary for a warrant, but not enough time to obtain a warrant beforehand. Such situations are called *"exigencies."* Cops may (with PC) search in a public place without a warrant to prevent evidence from disappearing. The exigency cannot be, however, of the cop's own making.

Emergencies

Another exigent exception to the warrant requirement is the protection of life and the rendering of aid. Such an exigency will allow the police to cross the 4th Amendment barrier. The most notable recent example of this was the LAPD homicide detectives climbing over the wall of O.J. Simpson's home, out of purported concern for his safety.

Conveniently overlooked at the show-cause hearing were the detectives' blatantly contradictory actions once inside the walls. Instead of feverishly searching the home for injured persons and looking upstairs, they milled about, sniffing for clues. Clearly, Mark Fuhrman (who had responded to Nicole's wifebeating complaints earlier) convinced the other detectives to rush over to O.J.'s. They had no real concern for O.J.'s safety, thus the "exigency" was a sham used to justify an illegal trespass and search. The prosecution managed to have the show-cause hearing judge (thoroughly out of her league and obviously overwhelmed) uphold the trespass, in the face of curiously lackluster defense objections. The jury seems to have seen through such (not to mention the perjury of Fuhrman) by acquitting after an astonishing blink of four hours. This acquittal will have major shock waves in law and police procedure.

Hot Pursuit

This is also an exigency. For sake of public safety, cops may (with PC) search a building and arrest without warrant a suspect who is dangerous and/or fleeing. Once a lawful arrest has begun, the cops are not rendered helpless merely because the suspect has fled to private property.

Border crossings

You've basically *no* 4th Amendment rights at the border. Agents can (according to *US v. Flores-Montano* of 2004) even remove and take apart your gas tank.

Search Incident to Lawful Arrest

As this is so closely related to an arrest, I discuss this search quite thoroughly in the Chapter 9, *The Arrest*. This search is ostensibly for protection purposes, but the cops love to find something extra after the arrest.

Automobile Searches

The *"automobile exception"* to the warrant requirement is well established. Since cars, planes, boats, etc. can be quickly moved while the police are obtaining a warrant, the courts have ruled that an exigency exists.

The cops may make a warrantless search of a car which was in motion, *or at least mobile*, when seized, and which they have PC to believe contains contraband or evidence of a crime—even if the car has been taken into police custody (*e.g.* the Lincoln search in *The French Connection*).

PC and the car's mobility must *both* exist *before* the seizure. If PC is discovered *after* the car is no longer mobile, or if the car was *not* mobile *before* seizure, a warrant is necessary.

Such a search may extend to any part of the car, including closed containers, which may contain the object of the search. (For example, a PC-based search for a stolen TV set cannot justify the opening of containers incapable of holding the TV set.)

Cops will often cleverly wait until a suspect brings a "dirty" container out of his house into a public area or his car where it can be seized without a warrant. As long as the contraband remains *inside* a house or its curtilage, the cops will need a warrant to search and seize.

Passengers subject to search because of PC on driver

In the 1999 *Wyoming v. Houghton* the Court ruled:

> *...that police officers with probable cause to search a car may inspect passengers' belongings found in the car that are capable of concealing the object of the search.*

By this ruling, the allowable scope of a *warrantless* automobile search based on probable cause is *broader* than the proper scope of a search authorized by a *warrant* based on probable cause! This is a *very* bad ruling, which **Thornton** (2004) complemented to make even worse.

Fifty years ago, Justice Jackson wrote something very timely:

> *The Government says it would not contend that, armed with a search warrant for a residence only, it could search all persons found in it. But an occupant of a house could be used to conceal this contraband on his person quite as readily as can an occupant of a car. Necessity, an argument advanced in support of this search, would seem as strong a reason for searching guests of a house for which a search warrant had issued as for search of guests in a car for which none had been issued. By a parity of reasoning with that on which the Government disclaims the right to search occupants of a house, we suppose the Government would not contend that if it had a valid search warrant for the car only it could search the occupants as an incident to its execution. How then could we say that the right to search a car without a warrant confers greater latitude to search occupants than a search by warrant would permit?*
> *We see no ground for expanding the ruling in the Carroll case to justify this arrest and search as incident to the search of a car.* **We are not convinced that a person, by mere presence in a suspected car, loses immunities from search of his person to which he would otherwise be entitled.** (332 U. S., at 587)

What about RVs and vans used as a home?

So long as they are *mobile* they will be treated as cars. However, RV's and travel trailers which are put up on blocks and connected to utility lines are most likely safe from the automobile exception. (If you're concerned about this, take photos of its nonmobile status to prove your case later. Anything you can do to *decrease* its ready mobility, such as blocking it in or adding skirting, will strengthen your case.) "Mobile homes" are not readily mobile and require a warrant to enter.

Consent
I discuss consensual searches only in the interest of thoroughness. My readers are presumed bright enough to *never* consent to a search. There is the sticky possibility, however, of a household member consenting to a search of your property without your knowledge or express permission, so I'll cover this.

The cops may conduct a search of property, even though they don't have a warrant or even PC, *if* they have obtained the prior consent of the one whose rights will be affected by the search, or of someone who has the right and the authority to act for the person whose rights will be affected by the search.

Consentor must have authority to permit the search
The consentor must have, or *appear* to have, authority over the premises. Such authority usually exists if he has joint access or control over the place/thing to be searched.

Examples of where such authority is *lacking* are:
✗ A landlord over a tenant's premises
✗ A hotelier over a guest's room during the rental period
✗ An general employee over his employer's premises
✗ An employer over his employee's exclusive premises
✗ A young child over his home without his parents

Examples of *unclear* authority are:
? Parents over room of adult offspring living at home
? Person of doubtful authority (guest, baby-sitter, etc.)

The courts have *disagreed* about:
? Dispute amongst those with equal rights over the premises. (Which prevails: one's consent or the other's refusal?)

Consent must be positive. Silence is *not* consent.
Vague acquiescence is usually insufficient. *"I guess so"* is not generally considered consent. It must be clear and positive.

The search is limited to the extent of the permission

The scope of the search is generally controlled by what the cop and consentor said. If the cop says that he thinks there is a gun in the car and the driver consents to a search, the cop may not search places obviously incapable of concealing a gun.

Administrative Searches

Heavily regulated business (*e.g.*, junkyards, pawnshops, firearms dealers, mining operations, etc.) are often subject to administrative inspections which require neither a warrant nor PC. Other licensed (privileged) professions are often subject to at least bookkeeping inspections. Anything seen by an official during a proper inspection is fair game.

This is an example of *"implied consent"*—a favorite tool used by government to get around the Bill of Rights. People are fooled into applying for licenses when such are often *not* truly mandatory, and the government gets to claim implied consent because of the actual voluntary nature of the license. Beware of licenses—they're really voluntary privileges with many strings attached. Read the fine print, for the devil is in the details.

Probation and Parole Searches

Probation and parole are voluntary agreements with the government in lieu of prison time. Part of the agreement for this release status is to be subjected to warrantless searches in which RAS (much less PC) is rarely required. Beware what you are asked to sign, and do so only after consulting a knowledgeable attorney.

In the 2001 ***US v. Knights*** the Court ruled that a probation condition that the defendant submit himself to warrantless searches is not limited only to searches with a *"probationary"* purpose. Knight had agreed to *"[s]ubmit his... person, property, place of residence, vehicle, personal effects, to search at anytime, with or without a search warrant, warrant of arrest or reasonable cause by any probation officer or law enforcement officer."*

SEARCHES NEEDING A WARRANT

The 9 pages of above exceptions aside, the only areas left which *do* require a search warrant is your home, non-licensed business, and *maybe* locked containers in your car. Every place else seems to fall into public plain view, a non-search, a *Terry* frisk, an exigency, some implied consent, a *"search incident to lawful arrest,"* or an *"inventory search."*

Though the police have historically whined that the warrant requirement hampers their work, such is clearly an ego-centrically-based exaggeration. Cops generally see only the trees and not the forest, and are understandably more concerned about criminals getting away than any blanket infringement of our rights. Many cops would prefer you to sacrifice your Liberty to give them tools to catch criminals. I suggest that such expediency is an extremely poor bargain.

Governments have caused (through their police and military) *thousands* of times more property damage, injury and death than mere criminals. Government has both a natural propensity to control and a legal monopoly on force—historically a disastrous combination. Consequently, I'd *much* rather suffer a small criminal class than a criminal *government*. Criminals I can more easily deal with.

So, the 4th Amendment provides a vital barrier to sweeping arrests and searches by purposely interposing the judiciary between the people and the executive. Just as a batter cannot call his pitches, the police cannot decide for themselves whether or not to enter your house. The judge is an umpire.

Probable Cause (PC)

> Probable cause to search is the existence of facts and circumstances that are enough to satisfy an officer of ordinary caution that a crime has been or is being committed, that the particular thing to be seized is reasonably connected to the crime, and that it can be found at a particular place.
> — *The Law Officer's Pocket Manual*, BNA Books

All real searches require PC (though not necessarily a warrant).

Constitutional requirements

The search warrant is valid only if pursuant to a sworn affidavit setting forth the facts establishing PC to search particular premises for particular items. Sufficient detail is required, especially when describing papers to be seized. "All records" is unconstitutionally wide and vague.

Timeliness of information and execution is crucial. Stale information invalidates a search warrant, and a search warrant, once obtained, must be promptly executed.

Mistakes in the drafting or execution of search warrants will be overlooked as long as they are "reasonable." This doctrine was created to bypass the exclusionary rule, and will be taken to terrifying new proportions over the next few years.

Contraband not mentioned in the warrant but found in plain view may be seized. Remember, as long as the police have a lawful reason to be somewhere, plain view applies.

Oral Applications for Search Warrants

Telephonic applications for search warrants are now generally permissible if the situation makes a written affidavit impossible or impractical. The feds may do so under Rule 41(c)(2) of the *Federal Rules of Criminal Procedure*.

The LAPD, for example, obtained a telephonic warrant to search O.J. Simpson's home, though I can't see how a written affidavit was even impractical much less impossible. I suspect abuse of these oral warrants, just as oral contracts are easily abused and misinterpreted.

USA PATRIOT Act "sneak and peek"

Section 213 of this Orwellian monstrosity authorizes federal agents to conduct covert searches of your home or office without notice until later. Up to 90 days later. That means you have little chance to point out (in time) deficiencies in the warrant or errors of its execution.

And, most notably, section 213 is not limited to terrorism investigations. It extends to *all* criminal investigations, and it is not scheduled to expire in 2005 as are several other sections.

During such a "sneak and peek" the feds will install keysniffer hardware/software in your computer to learn your email and PGP passphrases. Then they will remotely monitor your keystrokes, looking for PC to search and arrest.

I think any modern true American should have at least one laptop stored/used outside of home or office, and which is never connected to the Net.

Foreign national security threats have no 4th Amendment
Under section 218 of the Act, the *Foreign Intelligence Surveillance Act* of 1978 (FISA) was amended to allow wiretaps and physical searches without probable cause.

This section is scheduled to expire on 31 December 2005.

THE ARREST

Ideally, you *should* have handled things better and *avoided* the arrest in the first place. I will stress this point often. After an arrest, lawful or unlawful, matters generally go downhill from there, as you're in the custody of adversaries. You've been "captured" and are now a "POW." Unfun...

The best course of action

It's best to *avoid* an arrest, if such can be done without compromising your integrity and resoluteness. Don't take any crap, but it's generally foolish to expect granitelike repose of yourself 100% of the time. Remember, it's a "status thing" with most cops. If you give them utterly *no* way to save at least a *bit* of face, they'll often push matters to the next level—arrest. *Sometimes* it's wise to back down a notch.

Unless you've got strong public pressure on your side, vigilant legal help (for a writ of *habeas corpus*, especially), and unless you can take care of yourself on the inside, an arrest will probably go rather poorly for you. It's not a guaranteed horror story, but you should prepare for this possibility far in advance. I'm not trying to scare you into docility, but merely letting you know how it is.

If arrest is unavoidable

An inescapable by-product of our modern tyranny is that some of us may indeed become martyrs, but don't go *begging* for that honor through wanton recklessness.

> *God made the angels to show Him splendor, as He made the animals for innocence and plants for their simplicity. But Man He made to serve Him wittily, in the tangle of his mind! If He suffers us to*

> *come to such a case that there is no escape, then we may stand to our tackle as best we can. And yes, Meg, <u>then</u> we can clamor like champions...if we have the spittle for it. But it's God's part, not our own, to bring ourselves to such a pass. **Our natural business lies in <u>escaping</u>.***
>   — from the 1966 Best Picture *A Man For All Seasons*

Involuntary martyrdom looms heavily enough without you "mooning" the State. Besides, the "best" martyrs are *draftees,* not volunteers. Don't be a hothead, not even for the worthy cause of Liberty. Be *"wise as serpents and harmless as doves"* as Jesus advises in Matthew 10:16. Being wise is not necessarily being wimpy. *Cool* it and keep your wits about you. Fight on *your* terms and *your* ground, not theirs.

This goes double for you leaders in American Liberty—don't go salivating for some "hand to hand." This thing is a full-blown war, not a skirmish. We need wisdom, courage and stamina—not blind rage. We need you on the *outside*.

Legal basis for arrest / custody

Whenever a cop *"significantly restrains"* you, such *is* an arrest—even if he doesn't mean to actually arrest. Whether stemming from a warrant or exigent circumstances (or even a detention gone overboard), any significant restraint (arrest) *must always* be supported by *"probable cause"* (PC). Without PC, the cop may be liable for false arrest, and any evidence gathered is inadmissible in court (the "exclusionary rule"—now an endangered bulwark).

Defining *"probable cause"*

A landmark 1925 Supreme Court case (***Carroll v. US,*** 267 US 132) ruled that PC is based on facts sufficient to warrant a reasonable *person* to believe that somebody has committed a crime. (While it takes a cop to say what is *"reasonable suspicion"* because a suspect's actions could be innocently interpreted by others—*anybody* can recognize what is PC.)

The Colorado supreme court ruled in 1965 (***Gonzalez v. People,*** 177 Colo. 267) that *"one deals with probabilities."* A cop doesn't need the courtroom standard of *"proof beyond a reasonable doubt"* merely to arrest, he only needs reasonable probability.

What creates PC?

Generally, PC comes from evidence seen in *"plain view."* This doctrine also includes "plain hearing, smell, touch, etc." If the cop's five senses alert him to a crime, then he has PC. The important general standard is that the cop must personally *know* the factual situations involved. If he does not, then it is hearsay.

Can hearsay from an informant create PC?

While hearsay can *sometimes* establish PC, the standard is fairly strict. The cop must be able to explain:

❶ *why* the informant is a truthful, reliable person. (Special weight is given to "good citizens," victims of crimes, and cops. The courts do not normally believe: criminals, *quid pro quo* types, those with an "axe to grind," and the anonymous.)

❷ *how* he knows that the informant speaks from personal knowledge.

❸ *what* corroboration he has to confirm the informant's information.

When can a cop arrest with PC?

With PC, he doesn't need a warrant to arrest in public (on the road, at your public jobsite, on your front porch, etc.). When not in public (in your house or hotel room), he needs a warrant.

The cop's powers during a lawful arrest

He may use *"reasonable"* force to arrest—including up to deadly force, if necessary to prevent escape of a suspect whom the cop has PC to believe poses a significant threat to others.

You may be arrested for a mere misdemeanor offense

In the highly controversial 2001 ***Atwater v. City of Lago Vista***, the Court ruled that the Fourth Amendment does not forbid a discretionary warrantless arrest for a minor criminal offense, such as a misdemeanor seatbelt violation, punishable only by a fine. (In this case, a mother was needlessly arrested by a Texas cop for not wearing her seatbelt. She had to have a friend come pick up her crying children.)

In 100+ years of common law abrogation, non-violent misdemeanors involving utterly no "breach of the peace" have become arrestable crimes. The officer has personal discretion whether or not to simply cite the infraction, or haul you in. Don't make it a *personal* enough of a Scene for him!

However, the Court has also ruled (in *Blanton v. North Las Vegas*, 489 US 541) that in *"petty"* offenses punishable by less than 6 months you have *no* constitutional right to a jury trial! Not even if you are tried for a multiple of misdemeanors whose total punishment exceeds 6 months! Yes, treat you like a criminal with an arrest, but then deny your 6th Amendment right at trial. Great.

You can be arrested for *another's* contraband!

In 2003 *Maryland v. Pringle* the Court ruled that a rearseat passenger's drugs found in the armrest was sufficient probable cause to arrest a passenger in the *front* seat.

Beware who you drive with, else you could be caught up in a perceived criminal "common enterprise." Your companions could band together to rat you out, even if you are innocent.

On this note, do not pick up hitchikers—ever! Their odds of criminal records and/or activity is quite high, and you've no idea what they are carrying. (One southern California guy spotted a nubile young lass hitching home from school and picked her up. Almost immediately she turned to him and said, *"Give me all your cash, or I start screaming 'Rape!'"* You can probably figure out what he did. He lightened his load, both wallet and car. He doesn't pick up hitchhikers anymore . . .)

"search incident to arrest"   *Belton v. US*, 453 US 454

He may search your person and all places within your *"grabbable area."* This is often fruitful, so be sure that anything sensitive is securely stored in a strong, locked container. Your laptop should have very resolute privacy measures in place, such as PGP Disk and routinely shredded files and slack space.

More on this search shortly.

"inventory search"

If your car is impounded after arrest, it will very likely be thoroughly searched for "inventory" purposes. Ostensibly this is to protect the department against civil suits for property stolen while in their control. Realistically, it's a fishing expedition, and it's often very fruitful.

I read of a cocaine dealer (in the book *Dr. Snow*) who had a safe bolted to his trunk floor. The cops couldn't break in during the limited time they had his car. Pretty clever.

"minor bodily intrusion" (lovely oxymoron, that!)

He may order this during an *"exigency"* where a warrant is impractical, if such procedure is reasonable in nature and reasonably conducted, and he has: PC to arrest, *and "clear indication"* (between RAS and PC) that evidence will be found. The most common example is the drawing of blood to determine alcohol levels. The cop is on *very* tenuous ground here and must tread carefully. While I abhor irresponsibly drunk driving as much as the next, I am quite shocked over such independent powers—powers sufficient to order the piercing of skin with a needle. *"Minor bodily intrusion"* indeed! Only today's courts could dream up such an Orwellian oxymoron.

Your rights during an arrest

Pretty minimal. You have the *Miranda* right to remain silent, or to *become* silent at any time. You have the right to an attorney (free of charge) and may speak to him before and during questioning. Generally, you may not be subjected to a *"major bodily intrusion"* such as a cavity or surgical search or forced vomiting without a warrant unless a real *emergency* exists (imminent danger to life or limb).

PRACTICAL TIPS DURING ARREST

If arrested I would take a firm defensive stand by saying something like the following, **and then *shut up:***

> *I believe that I have a perfectly good defense, but I want to talk to my lawyer about it first. I understand that I have a right to remain silent, and a right to discuss my situation with a lawyer before saying anything to the authorities, and I intend to do just that. I intend to exercise my constitutional rights. Nothing personal, you understand.*
> — Univ. of Michigan Law Professor Yale Kamisar; *Supreme Court Review and Constitutional Law Symposium*, Washington, D.C., September 1982

I repeat: state the above and *shut up!* Your feet *had* their chance during contact, and *lost.* Your tongue had *its* chance during detention, and *lost.* **Now, *be quiet!***

What if it's clearly an unlawful arrest?

Though it seems only fair that one *should* be lawfully able to resist an unlawful arrest (and this is the case in some states such as Texas), such is not generally supported by the courts. In fact, resisting arrest (even an unlawful one) is an arrestable offense—so resisting a bad arrest will *give* it justification. **Therefore, do *nothing* to resist arrest.** "Resisting arrest" is the easiest thing for a bad cop to concoct, so beware. Cooperate physically or else he might include "resisting arrest" to cover himself.

Do not complain at the Scene about the bum arrest, rather save your allegations for later, *after* all the charges have been made and it's too late for him to include "resisting arrest" *ex post facto.* This is only being shrewd.

"search incident to lawful arrest"

The purpose for this search is to utterly ensure the cop's safety; to make certain that the arrestee has no hidden weapons. Also, the cop can seize any vulnerable evidence. There are three defining factors regarding this search:

❶ **Scope** (how *widely* he can search)—***Chimel v. California,*** 395 US 752 (1969)—limited this to the arrestee's person and any area under immediate control (the *"grabbable area"*).

❷ **Extent** (how *deeply* he can search)—***U.S. v. Robinson,*** 414 US 218 (1973)—allows a full field search of the above, including closed containers. Locked containers are generally off limits, as such require so much time to unlock/open that no immediate threat to the police can be reasonably presumed.

❸ **Timing** (*when* he can search)—must be *"contemporaneous"* with the lawful arrest, especially with regards to the surrounding area of the arrestee's car and home. Once in custody, these areas are generally off limits as the arrestee is presumably restrained from going for a weapon hidden in his glovebox, desk, etc. His *person,* however, may be searched even *after* arrest (*e.g.,* later at the police station), as he cannot be separated from his person (***People v. Boff,*** 766 P.2d 646 (Colo. 1988)).

He can now now search (according to ***Thornton v. US*** of 2004) even though you were *not* in your car when he initiated contact. (Hence, my previous tip of separating yourself from your car prior or during the stop is now likely ineffective in preventing a search incident to arrest. It's still worth a try, though. The cop may not be aware of ***Thornton***.)

A ***Terry*** frisk, however, of the same passenger compartment would still seem impermissible, assuming the exited occupant had no *"immediate control"* over such temporally or spatially.

Also, the cop may *not* conduct such a search unless he has *actually* arrested (in addition to merely detained) during those arrestable "cite-and-release" offenses (traffic tickets, jaywalking, having less than 1 oz. of pot, etc.) where he *may* arrest but chooses not to.

An implied lesson here is *not* to turn such a cite-and-release offense into an arrest. Unless your attitude is incredibly snotty or belligerent, you'll be cited and released. These discretionary arrestable offenses vary from state to state, so find out *prior* to being stopped.

Remember, these searches are incident to *lawful* arrest. If the arrest was *without* probable cause, or performed through either an invalid warrant or a valid warrant invalidly executed, or the arrest was not authorized for the offense—**the arrest and its incident search both fail.** Evidence from such is called *"the fruit of the poisoned tree"* and is inadmissible.

The cop's powers in a *"search incident to arrest"*

As you might have gathered, they're quite extensive. He may even search unlocked closed containers if he can prove that the arrestee *could* have gotten to them during arrest (***New York v. Belton,*** 453 US 455 (1980), the landmark case on this point). *Generally,* locked containers are out of bounds, though expect some future inroads to be made here. The so-called *"grabbable area"* can be *very* widely construed, usually including your car's passenger compartment, though *not* the trunk unless you are standing next to it during arrest and it's openable *without* a key (***Robbins v. California,*** 453 US 420 (1981)). Within these parameters, *anything* found is fair game.

Your rights during a *"search incident to arrest"*

Pretty thin.   Only major bodily intrusions (cavity and surgical searches) and locked containers require actual warrants.   The police are *not* supposed to move you about in order to increase the scope of their search (*U.S. v. Griffin,* 537 F.2d 900 (7th Cir. 1976)).

Practical tips during a *"search incident to arrest"*

The best advice is, obviously, to avoid being arrested in the first place. Barring that, I hope you'd taken my preparatory steps so that such a search turns up nothing useful to the police, like locking all your stuff in the trunk.

Barring *that*, the thought I have is not to widen your *"grabbable area"* by voluntarily changing locations (*e.g.*, going from sidewalk to your car, from outside your home to inside, or from inside one room of your home to another room.).

If an arrest seems likely, try to smoothly eliminate your property (car, home, business, etc.) from your *"grabbable area"* during the contact or detention stage—before actually being arrested. This area is defined *during* the actual arrest, not before, so you'll probably have a brief window of opportunity if the cop is not suspicious.

I did this very thing when stopped for speeding and knew that I had an outstanding warrant for an unresolved ticket. While the cop radioed me in, I discreetly secured my pistol and papers in a locked case. After cuffing me, he went through my car thoroughly but couldn't breach the locked case, to his disappointment. (After this, I learned to take earlier and more detailed preparations and *not* let old tickets go unresolved.)

The *"inventory search"*

This applies only to property on the arrestee's person, and in his impounded car (though generally not including locked containers).   The ostensible purpose is to protect your valuables, as well as cover the police in case of theft claims. But let's face it: the real, unstated co-purpose is to *snoop*.

The vehicle inventory search is legally complex and potentially detrimental to you, and that's why you *should* have pulled over in a private parking lot. The inventory search has been, predictably, abused by cops who use it for a pretext to search when they have no PC to search or can't search as thoroughly during a mere *"search incident to lawful arrest."*

Consequently, the courts generally require that less intrusive means than impoundment be used to secure the car. If it's legally parked, or may be legally parked close by, it can be locked up and left there. Or, it may be released to a sober passenger with a valid drivers license. Or, you might be able to call a friend and have it picked up quickly, though this will take some powerful persuasion on the cop (and maybe on your friend, too). I've gone through the impound thing twice, and it's a real hassle. Avoid it if you can.

If your car is either empty or packed to the roof, the cops may not even bother with an inventory search.

SEARCH OF CAR

LEGAL THEORY	REQUIREMENTS	Searchable Area
Consent	valid consent from person with *"joint access"* to car	anywhere consentor allows
Plain View	lawful presence; PC to believe evidence is crime-related; inadvertence	is not a search; may enter car to seize
Terry *frisk* (*Search Incid. to Detention*)	specific, explainable fear for safety *and* reason to believe weapon is in a particular reachable area of car	any area(s) where detainee could reach to get weapon
Probable Cause	PC to believe evidence is in car; warrant or exigency	areas authorized by warrant or exigency, where evidence could be located
Auto Exception	PC *and* mobility	anywhere evidence could be located
Search Incident to Lawful Arrest	valid custodial arrest	passenger area including unlocked, closed containers
Inventory Search	lawful custody	anywhere

SEIZURE OF CAR OCCUPANT

	MIN. EVIDENCE REQUIRED	COP'S POWER	SUSPECT'S RIGHTS
CONTACT	none	none (car must already be parked)	free to drive/walk away or ignore cop
DETENTION	traffic offense; or RAS of a crime	move driver to curb; ask questions; frisk with reasonable, explainable fear, demand name (though not ID if on foot)	free *not* to answer questions or give ID; free to go if no PC; can't be *"significantly restrained"* unless exigency
ARREST	PC that he committed crime	search incid. to arrest; handcuff; inventory of car; book	remain silent; make phone call; see an atty.; *habeas corpus*

AFTER THE ARREST: THE INTERROGATION

After the arrest, while being held

Do what they say. **Be polite, not snotty.** Such often lowers their guard, and may give you an unexpected advantage. Besides, politeness can go far as it's so uncommon in jail. Who knows?—a sympathetic soul might even do something kind for you. **A poor attitude *cannot help* in the slightest.** You're already in *custody* so don't make it worse. Once free, *then* you can get "uppity."

Say *nothing*. They're already so convinced of your guilt that they *arrested* you, remember? *Nothing* **you can say will change that. There is simply *no* talking your way out of it, so don't even *try*.** You might inadvertently give them something helpful. Also, you don't want to alert them to your legal strategies or any deficiencies in their case, however tempting it may seem to gain the upper hand, even if for a moment. Save this properly for later, as a *surprise*.

Sign *nothing*. Beyond an accurate inventory checklist of your belongings, sign *nothing*. Signatures always imply *agreements*. If the law truly requires something of you without your consent, then no signature is needed. **This goes *triple* for any form of deferred adjudication or probation.** The State offers these deals only when their case is weak. Stick it out for a *total* victory, if you can.

Beware of "favors." Behind bars it's a *quid pro quo* (this for that) world, and by accepting a "favor" you'll obligate yourself to returning one, usually at steep "interest."

Making post-arrest phone calls

You'll get three calls within several hours of booking, but the numbers are notated and jail phones are monitored, so beware. Unless you call your lawyer, consider setting up a relay instead of directly calling your home (which should be *private* to all but close friends and family). What I mean by a relay, is a message service or voice mail to take your "I've been arrested" call. From there a friend can pick up the message and make arrangements for you. The purpose of the relay is to keep your friends, home, business, etc. unknown to the authorities.

THE INTERROGATION

Arrestees should *never* answer questions and *always* demand an attorney. Though the police are then *required* to cease their questioning, this *doesn't* always happen—so you'll need to know how to resist a continued interrogation. A typical line is, *"Well, OK, you'll get your lawyer but first answer my question."* (The courts have held that answering questions after you've demanded your attorney cancels that demand.)

To avoid "reinventing the wheel" I'll paraphrase Jack Luger's *Ask Me No Questions—I'll Tell You No Lies* (from Loompanics) which has good, basic info.

Miranda a weak friend, and getting weaker

Courts have limited when police must give warnings, relaxed standards for what passes as a waiver of rights, said that a request for a lawyer must be explicit, and even allowed prosecutors to make moderate use of incriminating statements after a suspect has asked for a lawyer.

— Seattle Times, 29 March 1998, p.A16

If you cannot refuse to answer questions, then *Miranda* rights will not be your salvation. Keep your mouth shut!

Techniques of applying pressure
The first and most important task of the interrogator is to get you to *talk*. Without you, he has only a monologue. Remember, he *needs* you to talk. The State's case is incomplete and they want you to charitably fill it in. Don't worry if the police want to question you. **Be extremely nervous if they *don't*.**

Rapport
This is lull you into lowering your guard. He will be friendly, polite, and seemingly believing. Don't buy it! If he was your friend, he'd let you go home without a grilling.

Conditioning
This stage is to get you to answer questions in general. He'll begin with asking for routine, non-damaging information such as your name, address, and phone number. This is a seductive technique since there's no apparent harm in telling him what you think he already knows. Beware, he truly may *not* know much of the basic information. **Think *before* opening your mouth—and then, think *again*.** If you balk, he'll say it's only to verify his information. Call his bluff and ask to see his file on you and you'll personally correct any erroneous data.

He's also trying to establish a "baseline" of behavior as he notes your reactions. He'll carefully watch your eyes, expression, posture and body language. Later, when the critical questions come, he'll be alert for behavior changes to denote stress.

Repetition and Fatigue
He will try to wear you down by hammering the same questions again and again to force you: first to talk, and then to make mistakes and inconsistencies. Keep your polite silence!

Verbal Tricks
There are a few pat lines he'll try on you:

"I just need you to answer a few routine questions."
You'll hear this during the "conditioning" phase. "Routine" questions are *never* innocuous or unimportant.

"I'm only trying to help you."
Bullshit. Ask to be set free—*that's* "helpful!"

"I want to give you a chance to tell your side of the story."
Demand *their* version of the "story" without telling yours.

"What are you trying to hide?" (Presumes guilt.)
Reply, *"What are you trying to make me say?"*

"Innocent people don't mind answering questions."
Flatly reply that it's *because* you're innocent that you're not going to stick your head in somebody else's noose. (If they thought you were innocent they wouldn't be questioning you.)

"You'll feel better if you talk to me." (Presumes guilt.)
Reply that your conscience is perfectly clear.

"You lied before. Why should I believe you now?"
Simply deny that you've lied.

Intimidation
He could dispense with any rapport altogether and begin as a "hardass." Scowling, long periods of hopefully uncomfortable silence, staring you down, and good-cop-bad-cop ploys are to be expected. It's all melodrama, so don't let it get to you.

Squeezing for more
A basic technique is to say "and" whenever you stop speaking, which suggests that you have more to tell. Say, *"That's it. I've nothing else to say without my attorney."*

Expect predicated questions such as, *"When did you first start breaking the law?"* or something of that nature. Firmly deny the unstated assumption and clam up.

Single word questioning is used to goad elaboration. If you say that you were with a friend last night, he'll say, *"Friend?"* and simply stare at you. Say, *"Yes, friend."*

Bluff and Deceptive Tactics
Since the rack is out (generally), deception is in. At least half of any interrogation is pure bluff. Expect these lines:

"Your partner's already told us everything" or,
"We already know everything, so just confess."
Reply, *"Well, if so, then you don't need my story, do you?"*

"They just identified you."
This can be a lie or a totally faked demonstration. Call their bluff, *"Oh, darn! See you in court then."*

"This is your last chance for a deal."
Don't fall for this false sense of urgency. Such is B.S. unless the prosecutor signs a statement with your attorney there.

The Covert Interrogation
This takes place outside formal interrogations in settings which one would expect are safe.

Infiltrators and False Friends
They will try to worm into your life and get you to say something damaging. Suspect any new people, especially those who seem *too* agreeable, sympathetic and like-minded.

Undercover Cellmate
A cop poses as a criminal suspect and is placed in your cell. No *Miranda* warning is necessary during this ruse.

The Richard Jewell ruse
Remember the Atlanta Olympics security guard who found the backpack bomb? The FBI quickly suspected him of planting/finding it in order to appear a hero. So, they concocted the silliest of schemes: asking him to help them make an instructional video about suspicious packages. And to make the tape look like a real interview, said the agents, they wanted to read him *Miranda* rights. (A brilliant idea of FBI Director Freeh, who was covertly micromanaging the interview from DC) Jewell, no total dummy, smelt a rat and called his lawyer. He was eventually exonerated, and received a civil settlement from the FBI for leaking his name as a suspect to the media.

So, beware ruses of such nature. You're not obliged to help the authorities with anything like that.

COPING WITH THE SQUEEZE
With enough time and pressure, *anybody* will crack. Silence is the best route, for once you start answering questions the rest is easy for him. Many POW's know this personally.

How well can you resist?
How *vulnerable* are you to intimidation? You must examine your personality and honestly appraise yourself. If you are

easy to manipulate, suggestible and willing to talk—you of all people should *absolutely* demand a lawyer and shut up.

Can you stand silence with others, or do you feel a need to break the silence and say something?

Do you listen carefully when another speaks to you, or do you just wait for him to finish so that you can talk?

Do you crave attention, or prefer to be ignored?

Do you contact your friends as a rule, or do they call you? Do you need people more than they need you?

Are you suggestible? If someone says, *"Look at that,"* do you immediately turn your head?

Do you snap out your answers to questions?

Do you often need to explain and justify yourself?

Are you the "nervous" type, and do you show it by gestures and movements of the hands and feet?

How good is your resistance to discomfort?

Do you have a criminal record? This is vital in determining how investigators treat you.

What is your ethnicity? Certain races typically commit certain crimes, and he will look for stereotypical suspects.

What is your socioeconomic level? The more poor you are, the more you are assumed to be ignorant of your rights.

Avoiding emotional isolation

If subjected to a post-arrest interrogation, you will be separated from your friends and family. You won't have a lawyer unless you demand one. You'll be on the cops' turf, not your own. Realize this in advance and remember: the interrogation is only temporary. Stay silent and keep your wits about you.

Presenting a credible front

Most important is your overall image of respectability. A shady guy could actually tell the truth and be disbelieved, while a con-man exuding sincerity could be lying. Even though you should never answer questions, you should cultivate a *believable* air. This will likely reduce the length and ardor of the interrogation, and help cool their presumption of your guilt.

Eye Contact

Maintain eye contact. Don't let your eyes move differently when really grilled.

Speech

Regulate your tone and cadence. Avoid "ums" and "ahs."

Assertiveness

Be assertive without offensiveness. Such requires poise. Be polite, but don't take any crap or "bulldozing."

Body Language

Practice relaxing. Don't fidget, or tap your foot. Relax.

Preparation

If you're due for an interrogation, try to pre-enact the stress beforehand. If you keep a polite silence, you can't be tricked into hesitating, equivocating, or evading.

Tactical Resistance

Techniques are to deny-deny, shake your head whenever the interrogator begins to speak, and appear confused.

Exploiting Interrogator's Mistakes

Always have him give away more information than he gets. Analyze his questions to glean what he knows.

Don'ts

Don't volunteer *any* information

Supplying additional information leads only to additional questions. Make him ask you directly about something.

Dont display a *sullen* silence

Keep quiet, but be *cordial* (though not friendly).

Don't adopt an unusually calm, emotionless manner

This is unnatural and offensive to most people. Show reasonable, proper emotion (*e.g.,* indignation) for the situation.

Don't be a smartass during the interrogation

This conveys the attitude that you don't take him or his questions seriously, and makes it a Personal Thing.

Don't shoot your mouth off

Remember, silence is golden, even if others say it's yellow.

SOME FINAL TIPS

Two movies come to mind here: *A Man For All Seasons* and *The Usual Suspects*. On pages 203-5 of my novel *Molôn Labé!* is a great scene on handling a field interview.

If you are moved about and questioned by different cops, you should *restate* your position of silence and demand an attorney to *everybody who questions you.* Nobody in the entire building should be able to claim they "didn't know" of your invoking the Fifth Amendment. Sound like a worn record, *"I have nothing to say without my attorney present."*

If you wisely invoke your right to silence with demand for an attorney and are *still* subjected to an unlawful interrogation, this should be of *great* concern to you. Such post-silence interrogations are risky for the police, and you should strongly wonder *why* they are chancing a fat lawsuit.

Be *extremely* on guard here. If they belatedly realize their error, they might try to set you up while inside to pressure you into not going after them. Beware of something planted on you or in your cell.

I would immediately file a writ of *habeas corpus* to get before a judge and describe your unlawful treatment. If you are unconstitutionally prohibited from doing so, have somebody on the outside file on your behalf. You *must* bring swift and intense legal pressure to bear *immediately.* Go on the *offensive*—wars are *never* won through purely defensive postures. Try to get media attention if you're a "political" prisoner, or if the arrest is a pretextual sham. When the DA "feels the heat" he will probably "see the light." Good luck!

❖ 11

AT THE AIRPORT

The airport is the most vulnerable place one normally occasions. It is the epitome of controlled environments, in which you've voluntarily entered and thus given *"implied consent."* Nobody there has in mind your privacy or rights. You are under pressure to make your flight, defenseless, and under the gauntlet of 21st Century surveillance.

For the full treatment, experience Denver International Airport (DIA)—straight out of the futuristic movie *The Running Man.* The place literally sags with questions, cameras, cattle chutes, and that particular New World Order stench. (I'd personally rather risk the decennial terrorist or two than be subjected to such dystopian indignity.) DIA was so locally abhorred that many Denverites chose to drive the 60 miles and fly from Colorado Springs.

Today, after 9/11, all airports are about equally as odious.

The golden age of air travel is *over.* Commercial flight is now an Orwellian neo-fascist ordeal, as is simply motoring down the "free"way. First, they've got to make it a tribulation to travel, even domestically. Next, they'll try to bring regulatory grief to your porch. The goal? To make us miserable enough—hopeless enough—that we resignedly obey.

In warfare you try to deny the enemy his ability to:

Shoot   Move   Communicate

That is why we have so many restrictions on weapons, travel, and communication—and they are increasing every year. "Our" government sees us as its "enemy."

"Airport Security" (steel door on a grass hut)

Nick Monahan and his 7½ months pregnant wife Mary were "randomly" selected for a heightened search at the Portland International Airport on 26 October 2002. When his wife's breasts were touched and her swollen abdomen exposed in public by "airport security" personnel, Husband riled like a Man and verbally challenged such outrage. He was instantly swarmed by the domestic shock troops, arrested, and hustled off to a little room reserved for the non-sheeple. The Monahans had to drive to Seattle for a new flight (Nick was banned from Portland airport), but missed attending a friend's wedding. The airport Nazis did Nick a "favor" and declined to cite him with a felony. He paid a $309 citation.

But there's more to this needless saga. Mary's baby, likely from the trauma of its upset mother, had gone breech and wouldn't turn. As a first-time mother, Mary had an "untested pelvis" considered too risky for breech delivery. Now, a new mother who'd been planning a natural childbirth was forced to undergo a c-section. Meaning, hospital stay, epidural, catheter, fetal monitoring, stitches — everything she had been trying to avoid in the first place.

> I can never prove that my child went breach because of what happened to us at the airport. But I'll always believe it. Wrongly or rightly, I'll forever think of how this man, the personification of this system, has affected the lives of my family and me.
>
> There are plenty of stories like this these days.... There's no policy change that's going to save us. There's no election that's going to put a halt to the onslaught of tyranny. It's here already—this country has changed for the worse. **There is now a division between the citizenry and the state.** When that state is used as a tool against me, there is no longer any reason why I should owe any allegiance to that state.
>
> **And that's the first thing that child of ours is going to learn.**
> — www.lewrockwell.com/orig3/monahan1.html

The Monahans' son was born on 18 December 2002. No doubt he'll become a future reader of mine . . .

And all because the airport TSA now considers 7½ months pregnant women a "terrorist risk" (while not *daring* to discriminate against swarthy Middle-Eastern males). The most interesting thing about Monahan's experience was the attitude of the airport cops. They were genuinely perplexed at his anger, and opined that he was on drugs. Act like a Man and you're a whacko deserving of restraint and arrest.

There's a moral there ...

Tyranny is no longer poignant just for "extremists." At last, average folks are getting caught in the dragnet. Having run out of "black sheep" the feds are now nibbling at the main flock. *Good.* It's the only thing that can possibly wake up this slumbering nation. Bring on the oppression for *all* of us! Then maybe we'll finally stick a finger down our collective throat and vomit up this poison, versus spend another 20 years hugging the toilet, queasy and sick.

THE DRUG COURIER "PROFILE"

A primary risk you take at airports is being contacted and detained by the drug cops. Not because you are carrying drugs, but because you might unknowingly fit the "profile" of a courier. Even though this allegedly highly accurate "profile" results in only a 60% success rate (barely more than a coin toss), the courts still allow "profiles" to justify RAS and a detention.

I'm going to cover the "profile" inversely: instead of describing what it is, I'll tell you what behavior to avoid. Much of the following comes from *The Outlaw's Bible* by E.X. Boozhie, who compiled the first, and probably best, list. I include this information, not to assist drug traffickers, but to help the rest of you make your flights without undue hassle.

Avoid being attired:
- ✈ differently from other passengers
- ✈ inappropriately for the weather
- ✈ in the same clothes as when you left
- ✈ shabbily, or so as to reveal strange bulges

Avoid traveling alone, or:
- ✈ without luggage, especially on a long trip
- ✈ with empty, or untagged luggage
- ✈ with padlocks on your luggage
- ✈ with a shoulder bag
- ✈ with luggage inappropriate for your destination

Avoid flying:
- ✈ from a "drug source city"
- ✈ at off-peak hours
- ✈ on a round-trip ticket with a short layover
- ✈ on a ticket with a peculiar itinerary

Avoid purchasing your ticket:
- ✈ at the ticket desk
- ✈ on the same day as your flight
- ✈ with cash (particularly small bills)
- ✈ changing flights enroute

Don't act suspiciously, like:
- ✈ scanning, or cloak-and-dagger stuff
- ✈ cautious, hesitant, nervous, or furtive behavior
- ✈ inordinate haste, or killing time inappropriately
- ✈ going directly to the telephone
- ✈ avoiding your travelling companions

When returning home from abroad:
Avoid making short trips abroad, or returning directly from a "drug source country"

With regard to your airline ticket:
- ✈ Avoid purchasing it with cash
- ✈ Know when/where/how it was purchased

Avoid travelling:
- ✈ alone, particularly if you're a Latin woman
- ✈ with only a small piece of luggage

Don't exhibit:
- ✈ Extreme passivity/indignation, or nervousness
- ✈ Talkativeness or extreme helpfulness with Customs

Appear to be dependent on checks and credit cards
- ✈ Carry a checkbook, traveler's checks and credit cards
- ✈ Avoid carrying large sums of cash

Have a *plausible* story if asked by US Customs
- ✈ Have a sight-seeing itinerary if claiming tourism
- ✈ If on business, be able to prove it with details

Misc. tips of my own:

A combination of several of these "profile" characteristics will probably cause a DEA agent to accost you to "ask a few questions." Ask if you are being arrested or detained! Politely ask to see his credentials. After writing down his name and ID#, return it, politely refuse his "invitation" and walk away. He must either detain or arrest to prevent you from leaving. He will want to see your ID and ticket. During contact and detention, you may (and should) *refuse.*

If your bag is detained and you don't want to be around when they sniff it, firmly state your possessory right to it, explain that you'll return with your attorney to retrieve it, and leave the airport. Cash and other sensitive items you should keep on your person, anyway.

To foil or delay searches put your cash and papers in a Priority Mail Tyvek envelope affixed with postage and safe address. Only a postal inspector with PC can open it. *Really* sensitive stuff should be mailed ahead, anyway.

Guns may be legally transported in your check-through luggage if they're unloaded, in a locked hard case, and declared to the ticket agent. You'll sign an orange tag which reads, *"I declare, as required by the Code of Federal Regulation 108.11, that the firearm(s) being checked as baggage is (are) unloaded:"* (Expect to be searched much more frequently if you fly with a gun. You may want to UPS it ahead c/o yourself.)

Before landing from overseas, fill out *two* US Customs cards identically. On the ground, if you are accosted by a roving Customs agent who views you suspiciously, he will ask for your card, and scribble some cryptic notation—alerting the desk agent to thoroughly search your stuff and really grill you. Pocket that card and present the *other* one, which hasn't any such notation. (A tip from personal experience! BTP)

THE TERRORIST PROFILE

About half of the 9/11 hijackers were *already* on the FBI watchlist, and most of them booked their flights on *credit cards.* So, I'm kinda wondering why FBI agents weren't there at the gates to intercept them.

The typical terrorist hijacker has historically been an Arabic male between 18 and 40 years of age. To focus on such men at airport is not profiling, but (as Ann Coulter well put it) *"a description of the suspect."*

But please do not worry if you fit such a profile, for you will be studiously left alone during the Iroquois gauntlet of "airport security." Instead, the TSA will focus on your grandmother, children, or your pregnant wife. This phenomenon is now *so* widespread that I'm hearing such stories from random strangers in the checkout line. (One woman, white/blond/blue eyed, endures secondary security *every* time she flies, yet an Arabic friend of hers is never bothered.)

TSA "WATCH LIST"

The *New York Times* had an interesting story about this on 2 November 2004 (p.C8). The list (which replaced Capps-II) is thought to include more than 40,000 names from at least nine government databases. A few thousand are on the "no-fly" list, while the rest ("selectees") are slated for detailed questioning prior boarding.

How can you become a "selectee"? Oh, it's very easy. Pay for your ticket with cash, book a seat at the last minute, fly one-way instead of round-trip, or arrive at the airport without bags. Or, more vaguely, if you have *"a pattern in something* [you] *have done in the past that merits future scrutiny."* Great.

Your only hope in getting removed from the watch list is file a "disparity claim" with the TSA ombudsman. You will be emailed a "Passenger Identity Verification Form" requesting copies of your driver's license and voter registration card, as well as height, weight, and eye color. (Then, be prepared to wait.)

If you can drive, do so. Flying really has become a gross indignity, and the American people have accepted it.

AT THE CHECKPOINT

These include random sobriety checkpoints, license checks, Border Patrol checkpoints fixed miles inside the USA borders, agricultural checkpoints, etc. If you wander in one of these ongoing fishing expeditions, the courts will "reason" that you *chose* such over alternative routes. As explained in Chapter 7, the "Checkpointeers" may ask you their questions (which you are *not* required to answer), but they *must* allow you to pass—unless they have RAS to detain or PC to search or arrest.

Not all, however, will let you go so easily. INS agents are the worst offenders. I once had to pass through one of their "temporary" Border Patrol checkpoints located far inland. While they are quite fixed and elaborate, the Supreme Court ruled in *U.S. v. Martinez-Fuerte*, 428 US 543 (1976) that they cannot be operated 365 days—thus the "temporary." Anyway, after ascertaining that I was an American, "GreenMan" asked where I was headed. *"North,"* I boredly answered.

INS:	*"Well, I know that, but what's your destination?"*
me:	(Indignant:) *"That's a rather personal question!"*
INS:	(Now hostile:) *"What's in your trunk?"*
me:	(Firmly:) *"Lawful personal property."*
INS:	*"Open it!"*
me:	(Flat:) *"No."*
INS:	(Leaning into my face, menacingly:) *"No?"*
me:	(Even more flatly, almost yawning:) *"That's correct, no."*

By that time his partner had joined him and they barraged me with *"What's in your trunk? Whose car is this? Where did you come from?"* and questions of similar ilk. I cut them short with:

me: (Resolute:) *"Gentlemen, I am a law-abiding American going about my lawful business. I am carrying no contraband. I've committed no crime. Unless you can state probable cause to the contrary for the benefit of my tape-recorder here, I shall be on my way."*

That micro-cassette recorder to ICs was like a cross to Dracula. They totally deflated and backpedaled their way out:

INS: (Effusive:) *"Oh, hey, we weren't trying to hassle you! Haven't you ever been through here before?"* (Translation: *"Why don't you whimper at our every command?"*)
me: (Stern:) *"Yes, I've passed through here before, and I cannot recall having been treated with such disrespect!"*

All they wanted right then was for me to drive away, which I did amongst their profuse *"Bon voyages."* **The lesson: know your rights and *assert* them.** Americans need to stop rolling over and peeing on their bellies as cowering puppies! **Enough of this wimpery!** Men—start acting like Men! Ladies—*shame* these thugs into treating you as ladies.

Avoid driving near Canadian and Mexican borders:
✗ an enclosed truck, van, or station wagon
✗ with numerous passengers
✗ on infrequently travelled roads

When crossing borders, avoid driving:
✗ alone, especially if you're an elderly man
✗ a rented car, or with out-of-state license plates
✗ an empty car

Beware the federal areas

Military bases, National forests and parks, Indian reservations and federal offices are all bits of *"United States"* territory wherein the Bill of Rights barely exists, if at all. (I cover this in the chapter *Our Dwindling Rights*.) Whenever you enter the "federal zone" you are technically amidst another country within the USA borders.

Try to avoid these areas if you can. If you can't, then prepare yourself and your property *very* thoroughly. The federal zone is hostile territory, so beware.

RED LIGHTS ARE FLASHING

Make no furtive or sudden moves. Stay *calm*.

Cops love to closely follow a "hinky" driver in hopes of rattling him. Stay cool and collected. Don't start rearranging your car's entire interior—that should have been done before setting out. Quickly and smoothly secure any unlawfully carried weapons, lock up your personal effects in the briefcase, and perform the next bit, if you can.

If you're *about* to be pulled over, *beat him to it*

The less you drive in his presence, the fewer "traffic infractions" he can allege and the fewer pretexts he can concoct to detain you. (In fact, I make a rule of not allowing the police behind me, not even for a few blocks. I keep them in *front* of me.)

Act like you don't see him, pull over at some business, get out, lock up your car, and walk away. Act surprised when he pulls up behind you. By separating yourself from your car *before* he lit up his lights you've made it more difficult for him to involve your car and contents in his snooping.

When pulled over, do so in a private parking lot

The reason for this is that if you *are* arrested, your car can possibly remain there, rather than suffer a *"search incident to arrest"* or be impounded for an *"inventory search"* If you've no cell phone, try to pull over near a pay phone. That way, if the Scene turns dicey and your arrest is likely, you can call a friend to come fetch your car and let him know where you will be taken. If possible, ask the store manager for permission to leave your car on his lot until your friend arrives shortly. (Allay his fears with the explanation that it's merely an unpaid ticket causing all the hassle.)

Have any cover story already prepared

While I don't recommend answering personal questions, a cover story can be good to have. The basic thing is to keep it simple, benign, and in *agreement.* You're on your way to the mall to buy some sheets, whatever. My own pat story is coming from K-Mart where I was looking for, with no success, some metric allen bolts. (There's even a missing such bolt under my hood. It's perfectly benign *and K-Mart never has them.*)

"Where am I going? Well, to some hardware store; any suggestions, Officer?" Do you see the beauty in that? I'm on a routine, boring mission which explains where I've been and where I'm going. Make up your own, like searching for an exotic brand of hot sauce (which nobody carries). It's defensible, different enough to sound true, yet offers *nothing.*

You want to sew up the Scene quickly and firmly, leaving him with no secondary inquiries to make. Remember the highway patrolman who pulled up while I was unsticking a choke? I initiated the confrontation, explained in 8 seconds—leaving the issue closed—and walked back. Nothing about my car or demeanor was suspicious, so he had nowhere to go but away.

You are *not* going to: the airport, the gun range, a friend's house, etc. All these destinations invite further questions: *"Really, where are you flying to?"* or *"Oh, so you have guns in this car?"* or *"Which friend is that?"* Once you start stammering to these follow-up queries, you're in for a *real* grilling. Have a simple story which contains its own beginning and end. Leave him no place to go. And make sure that your passenger can play along.

Start the "clock" ticking

Time is not on his side, and he's banking on you not knowing this. If your watch has a stopwatch feature, click off when his lights begin flashing. He's got an easy 20 minutes. After 20 minutes it becomes increasingly difficult to justify detaining you (especially when you don't operate as your own enemy). If the detention looks flimsy in court, a cop will usually understate the length of detention. Forty minutes becomes 25, and 15 minutes was "only 5 to 7." Have credible evidence to counter this eventuality.

While I've rarely been held for as long as even 20 minutes, it's happened. If he seems to be stretching it out regardless of his time window, remind him that the "sand is running out" and point to your stopwatch. *"Officer, we both know that you can't detain me forever. Shall we be on our ways now?"*

Get out coolly and lock your car door behind you

If he wishes, the cop will order you *out* of the car. His power to do so was held in ***Pennsylvania v. Mimms,*** 434 US 106 (1977) and other cases.

Get out naturally without waiting or asking. By doing so, you've separated your person from the interior of your car (which otherwise is considered within your *"grabbable area"*). Since the courts have held that the cop's safety is paramount to your 4th Amd. right, the cop can ***Terry*** frisk your person and any area functionally within your *"grabbable area"* (*e.g.,* an unlocked car, nearby surroundings, etc.) for weapons. By locking your door, you've made the passenger compartment almost as inviolate (there's always *"plain view"* PC) as the trunk.

Do recall, however, that a *"search incident to arrest"* will breach the passenger compartment, and likely the trunk.

It is *not* guaranteed that you will always be allowed to exit. In fact, a particular court case (***People v. Harrison,*** 443 N.E.2d 447 (1982)) ruled that the cop *may* legally order you back *into* your car. Such can be a clever move on his part since it automatically increases your *"grabbable area"* and thus the area of a ***Terry*** frisk or *"search incident to arrest."* You want to be *out* of the car for the same reason a snooping cop wants you *in*. Quickly getting out will make many cops suspicious. Get out *coolly*, and return *without a fuss* if he tells you to.

I had an interesting opportunity to test this years ago:

Boston's real-life incident #1

A rather shrewd highway patrolman in an unmarked car managed to pace me at 75+ and thus not activate my radar detector. I quickly secured my belongings as described, pulled over, got out, locked my door behind me, and walked back. (The interior of my car was spotlessly clean and totally empty. My

---

trunk, however, was packed with personal belongings.) To my surprise, he asked me to wait in my car. (I couldn't remember this *ever* having happened. I always get out and leisurely walk back.) Anyway, the Scene went like this:

me: *"I'd rather wait outside. My AC doesn't work and I'm hot."*
Cop: *"Well, I still need you to wait inside your car."*
me: *"Look, I've been on the road all day, I'm hot and I'm getting cramped up in there. I'd rather wait outside and stretch my legs."*
Cop: *"Yes, but please just wait in your car. This won't take long."*
me: *"But why can't I simply walk around and stretch my legs?"*
Cop: (Annoyed:) *"Sir, it's for safety's sake. Please wait inside."*
me: (Pushing the issue, out of curiosity:) *"Well, I'm not concerned with my safety, and if you're concerned about yours, you can give me a* Terry *frisk—I'm not armed or anything."*
Cop: (Clearly surprised at my firmness and knowledge of *Terry*:) *"Sir, I'm not going to tell you again! Get back in your car!"*
me: (Really pushing it now:) *"Is this a request or legal demand?"*
Cop: (Now annoyed and suspicious:) *"It's a legal demand. What is this—is there something in your car you don't want me to see?"*
me: (Walking back to the car:) *"No, I'm just tired of being cooped in there, that's all. Also, I wasn't sure if you were asking me or telling me."*
Cop: (On a hunch:) *"You wouldn't have a gun in there, would you?"*
me: (Cool:) *"As I said, officer, I'm not armed. I just preferred to be outside and walk around in the fresh air."*

Obviously, I brought on his suspicion by pressing the issue of staying outside. When he saw that I had to unlock the door to get in, he was *really* on alert. Remember, this was an *intentional* test case, with full expectation of his likely reaction. I gave him my paperwork through the driver's window, he radioed a check on me, and (as I later realized) requested backup. After about 7 minutes he returned, and said I could step out of my car. I got out, again locked the door behind me and walked back. To my initial surprise, he explained that he was going to merely give me a warning on the speeding. As I quickly understood, this was not out of generosity, but to soften me up for the next stage:

Cop: (Handing me the warning ticket:) *"Here you are. Please watch your speed. Say, would you mind if I looked under your seat?"*
me: (Unemotional:) *"What would you be looking for?"*
Cop: *"I believe you have a pistol under your seat."*

me: (Not flustered, but a touch indignant:)   *"As I've already said, officer, I'm not armed. I have nothing to do with drugs; I have no contraband in the car. There's nothing there to concern you."*

Cop: (Somewhat taken aback:) *"So you're refusing consent?"*

me: (Pleasant, though firm:) *"That's right. I never waive my rights , and in fact, I'm a bit insulted by all this."*

Cop: (Cajoling:) *"Oh, you wouldn't be waiving your rights! You'd just be cooperating! Who told you it's waiving your rights?"*

me: *"My attorneys. I travel on business and they counseled me on this a long time ago, because I was curious. There's nothing to be gained by me waiving my rights, even if I have done something wrong—which I haven't."*

Cop: (Realizing consent was impossible, and "getting tough":) *"You know that I can call for a drug-sniffing dog, don't you?"*

me: (Calling his bluff:) *"Oh? How will a drug-sniffing dog alert to a gun, which is just a piece of steel?"*

With that he marched back to his radio to call for a dog. Just then a colleague of his showed up, and I then realized that he had been on his way minutes earlier. The second cop was very cool and we made pleasant conversation. *Many* times have I indirectly softened up a ticked off cop by simply being polite with his colleague. If the first cop is an IC or RC, try to bring out "Good Cop" in his partner. Once, a *real* RC (who was planning to set me up) was so incensed by my casual attitude that his partner actually took him aside and talked some sense into him. Happily, a very dicey stop was defused.

After 5 minutes, the first cop returned and said that I was free to go as the dog was too far away (to arrive within a *"reasonable"* time of 20-30 minutes).

A word of advice here: when being released after a heavy Scene, don't become overtly happy and relieved—that implies guilt. **Soften, *but don't cancel*, your aura of indignation. Make *them* glad to be rid of *you*, not vice versa.** Don't blow your release by getting all giddy.

Anyway, I extended my hand, shook his, thanked him for the warning on the speeding ticket and said:

me :   *"Look, you haven't missed anything here. I'm not up to anything. I just believe in standing up for my rights. It's nothing personal with you, OK?"*

Cop: (Holding back a grin:)   *"Yeah, well, let me explain the laws around here regarding a pistol in your car. You can carry in your car as long as it's in a holster and left either under your seat or in the glovebox."*
me: (If so, then what was this whole Scene about?, I wondered to myself.) *"Well, Officer, I can assure you that if I were to travel with a pistol in my car, it would be secured exactly in the manner you just described."*

He and his partner couldn't help but chuckle at that. I bid them good day and drove off. In retrospect, it couldn't have ended better: I avoided a search *and* got off with a warning.

The lesson here is to learn *beforehand* if the cop can order you back to your car. (I didn't know and purposely pushed it to find out.) If they can, get out anyway, and *if* they order you back, comply without a fuss. Your car interior *should* be able to withstand a frisk or search, anyway—if necessary.

If he seems to want to go through the interior, try to lock and close the door behind you as you get out.

If, in your city/state, carrying a gun in your car is lawful, then consider this sudden idea: Secure your pistol as described in Chapter 4, get out and lock the door behind you. If he orders you back inside, reply, *"Oh, I thought you'd feel safer with me outside and my pistol remaining inside the car."* For him to *then* order you inside would contradict any purported concern for his own safety. If he demands to check out the pistol, reply that carrying an unloaded and locked pistol is not unlawful, and thus your pistol shouldn't be any concern of his. You will *not* show him your pistol, nor will you get back in your car *until* your business is completed and he has gone.

I've never tried this, but it would *seem* to thwart any otherwise lawful order to return to your car (as such would, in this case, *increase* the cop's risks—not reduce them). Any readers with the guts to try this and report back, will have their experiences discussed in the next reprint of this edition.

Another incident worked *better* because I *had* gotten out:

Boston's real-life incident #2

I was on the highway doing about 75 mph and gradually overtook a trashed out pickup. "Hardass" got his stupid ego involved, passed me and then resumed his 65 mph. I kept my speed constant and passed him. When he passed me *again,* I got tired of the cat and mouse, flew by, outdistancing him by a mile when a highway patrolman (hiding beyond an overpass) zapped me at 80 mph.

I pulled over rather quickly and got out just as he had stopped. The junker pickup roared past just as the HP and I met. HP's eyes bugged out at the sight of my holstered pistol (open carry is lawful in that state). I calmly admitted to speeding and explained that it was to outdistance the weird guy in the beatup truck. I further explained that his license plate was attached in a suspicious manner, probably to make it hard to read. The HP, once presented with this reasonable story, took off! Though I was clean-cut and polite, I was armed and I think that he merely wanted to leave.

Your actions and body movements are crucial

Make sure your hands move normally, and keep them seen at all times (out of your pockets). Relax and let your arms hang naturally. Crossed arms are a subliminal sign of defiance. Do *not* light up a cigarette, especially at night. Drunk drivers typically do this to hide their alcohol breath.

Be pleasant and find out *why* he stopped you

This assumes you weren't stopped for doing 100 mph in a school-zone. If the reason is obvious, *don't ask* because you'll come off as a real smartass. On this point, the funniest example I ever saw was the opening 3 minutes of some TV show. A Porsche 928 led about 15 cops on a horrific high-speed chase all over L.A. When finally cornered in a parking garage, a cop guardedly approached the driver's tinted window. It rolled down to expose a very distinguished older gentleman in an expensive suit, with a beautiful young woman. Utterly smooth, he asked, *"Is there a problem, Officer?"*

If suspicious, cops don't like to immediately tell you why they stopped you. What you don't know is leverage against you, and they are loath to give up that leverage. You must quickly find out why you've been stopped to understand how the Scene is likely to play.

I don't care much for the tired, old line, *"Is there a problem, Officer?"* Try something totally disarming and innocuous: *"Did I do something wrong, Officer?"* The cop may blurt out the real reason for stopping you. If the nice, innocent approach doesn't work, then you'll probably have to be hardnosed. Give nothing until he shows a bit of courtesy and explains.

Once you know, defuse his suspicion and seek to leave. Once you've offered a perfectly reasonable explanation for your behavior, you've pretty much terminated the basis for detention. You're now on the higher ground. Don't budge by answering more questions. Keep seeking to leave. (If you don't, remaining *could* appear voluntary.)

Don't be in an obvious hurry to get out of there

Gushing relief and thanks is only suspicious to a cop—it makes him wonder what he *really* missed. Save the rejoicing for later. On the flip side, don't *overdo* the "ain't-no-thing" bit. Once released, don't hang around and make conversation, figuring you're in clear so why not "rap with the Man." *Slide on outta there!* You're not safe until you're gone.

"NO, YOU'RE NOT FREE TO GO!"

Once your paperwork has been returned with his lecture or ticket (or both), you're free to go unless he has additional RAS to detain you further. **If this happens, be *extremely* on guard.** For some reason, you're likely on a short, slippery rope to arrest. I've got a couple of stories:

Boston's real-life incident #3

I was on a road trip (a working vacation with research materials and computer to write *Good-Bye April 15th!*). The day had not started well; I had overslept an early morning departure, missed breakfast, and was running very late for a meeting 300 miles away. And then I got nabbed on the highway for 75+ mph, just a half hour from my destination. That capped off an already rotten morning. The cop routinely wrote up my ticket, handed it to me with my license and matter-of-factly asked if he could look in my trunk.

me: (Cold:) *"No, you may not. I don't have time for it, and there's nothing inside to concern you."*
Cop: *"It'll only take a minute."*

me: (Annoyed:) *"I don't have 'a minute.' I'm late already, which is why I was speeding, remember? I need to be on my way now."*

Cop: *"No, stay right here. You appear nervous to me, and I think you're hiding something."* (Even though this was insufficient basis for RAS, he claimed he had RAS, so I had to remain.)

me: (Extremely annoyed:) *"I'm not nervous! I'm just tired, hungry, and I don't like speeding tickets, much less being treated like a criminal."*

Cop: (Unmoved:) *"Just stay here, I'll be right back."* (He then went back to his car, and returned after being on the radio for a good 5 minutes.) *"OK, here's the deal. You know and I know that I can't search your trunk without either your permission or probable cause. So, what I've done is call for the drug dog, and if he alerts to the presence of drugs that gives me probable cause, and I will search your car."*

me: (Cool anger:) *"I wish I could say that you're 'barking up the wrong tree,' but you're not even barking up a 'tree!' Taking drugs to ____* (a major "drug source city") *is like taking french fries to McDonalds! It's ridiculous! Since you've pushed this so far, I'm going to get my camcorder and film this whole thing."* (This was during the uproar over Rodney King's beating.)

Cop: (Going absolutely ballistic:) *"You will not film this, you will not record this! I'm in control of this scene!"*

As I didn't then know my legal grounds on this point, I acquiesced. What I've since learned is that as long as you don't interfere with their duties, you've got a perfect right to video the Scene. Heck, if the police get to have TV's *Cops* film their Scenes, why can't you?

Anyway, after only 5 minutes a deputy arrived with his dog. He and the cop huddled for a moment, and then the deputy walked over leading his dog. He started at my driver's door and ambled back to the trunk, subtly touching the lid along the way. (This is clever and shabby trick. What they do is first touch a bag of pot in their pocket, then slyly transfer the scent onto whatever they want the dog to "alert." It's guaranteed to create probable cause.) Predictably, the dog alerted to my trunk.

Cop: (Smug:) *"Did you see that? He alerted to the presence of drugs in your trunk. I now have probable cause to search it. Open it."*

me: *"Nice trick. Well, you all may have just concocted probable cause, but I don't have to help you in this. I will not open my trunk, as such may be construed as consent."*

Cop: (Giving me a pretextual *Terry* frisk to find the trunk key:)   *"Now you're not under arrest here, I'm just patting you down for weapons."*

About this time (without a second radio call, thus confirming my suspicions of a setup) a DEA agent drove up, drooling over another prospect. He was a stunningly obese 300 pounder, sweating more than Charles Laughton in a sauna. (He was the model for the DEA agent "Oilturo" in my *Molôn Labé!*) The three of them emptied out my packed trunk (mainly full of books, which caused them some bafflement). After conferring with the other two cops, he waddled over and tried to "Good Cop" me (like I've got the IQ of salad).

DEA: *"Howya doin? So, you like camping?"* (I had gear in the car.)
me: (Bored:) *"Don't talk to me like I'm some hick at a bar."* (He asked some more questions which I either ignored or deflected.)
DEA: (Angry:) *"Well, you won't cooperate! You're just an *sshole!"*
me: (Icy:)   *"I was under the impression that your agency had standards for language and* (looking at his big beer gut) *physical fitness."*

With that he stomped off. By now, my whole trunk's contents had been emptied and laid out behind my car in two rows, with the dog doing a figure eight through them. He alerted to nothing. Frustrated, they had the dog jump in the trunk, and he didn't alert to the empty trunk, *either*. Now, *really* frustrated, they started pawing through my bags (even though they did not have *specific* probable cause to search through any of them).

Not finding anything, they opened my passenger door (*without* the dog having first alerted to the passenger interior). The dog leapt in over my color monitor and kicked it out with his hind legs, sending it rolling down the shoulder. He then tore around my front seat and dash, trashing it with his muddy paws and breaking an expensive pair of sunglasses. The back seat was piled to the ceiling, so he couldn't get back there. Since his actions were inconclusive, they then called for a *second* dog.

It arrived with the county sheriff himself, leisurely climbed on the front seat and proceeded to have a nap. Now, the four cops and two dogs are looking pretty stupid. It's become a "status/penis thing" and they're now *really* intent on finding some drugs in my car to justify the whole Scene. This is where I got concerned that they would plant some. (Don't get your sensibilities in a pinch; bad cops plant stuff if they're desperate.)

me: *"This has obviously been a mistake, and I think even you realize it by now. As I said, I've nothing to do with drugs. The only drugs that could be found in my car are those that were put there."*

They didn't like this at all, and proceeded to empty out the interior, pull up the back seat, open the hood to look in the air cleaner—the works. Traffic is now diverted around us because of 80 feet of orange pylons behind us. It's a Scene.

To illustrate how incompetent these guys were, listen to this: They found my pistol (which was lawfully owned and carried), cleared the chamber, called in the serial number, set the pistol on top of a bag not four feet away, *turned their backs on me and went back to going through my car!* Had they done this to the wrong guy, he could have easily grabbed the pistol, hit the slide release and gunned them down! These were *sloppy* cops.

So, they've gone through the entire car and all my bags, finding zip. I'm disgusted and the look on my face is one would have after catching some pervert masturbating in the park. Without a word, they began putting the stuff back in my car.

me: (Disgusted:) *"'Thank you,' but I'll do that! I think you've handled my things enough for today."*

I packed it all back up and walked over to them, sullenly congregating like the jackals they were.

me: *"Well, had enough? Am I free to go now?"*
Cop: (Flat:) *"Yes."*
me : (Outraged:) *"'Yes?' That's all you've got to say after all this? No, 'Our mistake—we apologize.'? No 'Sorry for breaking your stuff and wasting 45 minutes of your time, Sir.'?"*
Cop: (Suddenly indignant:) *"Hey, we're just doing our job!"* (Ah, the old "Nuremberg defense!")
me: *"Hah! Gentlemen, before this incident I thought pretty highly of the police. Now, I don't. You're squandering the very thing you need—the good faith obedience of the American people. Honest folks aren't going to take this crap forever, and someday you'll be in for a rude awakening! Go catch some criminals and leave the rest of us alone!*

On a happy note, I contested the ticket and demanded a jury trial. Word got around the courthouse that I was pretty hot and that a civil suit was likely. They dropped the matter. So, no fine *and* I got an educational experience from it all. *Heh!* Did I do anything about this outrage later? No. Except to write this book. That's the best justice for those hyenas.

What would I do differently today? A few things. I would have embarked on the road in a better frame of mind. I would have been more alert and probably avoided being nabbed for speeding. I would have forbidden the dog handler to touch my car. I would have indeed camcorded the search. I would have gotten everyones' name and badge number. I would have filed a lawsuit for a groundless detention. Generally, I would have raised a real stink. They had *their* fun, so why not have *mine?*

Are you ready for another *"No, you're not free to go"* story?

Boston's real-life incident #4

Late at night I was stopped for speeding by a highway patrolman (HP). In my experience, minority cops more often have a "chip on their shoulders" and this Hispanic guy didn't "disappoint." He was very near to being a Rogue Cop.

While I tried to located my license in my wallet, he got impatient after about 5 seconds, exclaimed, *"Give me that!"* and grabbed for my wallet! I won the brief tug-of-war, and from then on both of us were pretty angry. He then asked to search my motorcycle saddlebags (which were locked).

When I indignantly refused, he tried to open them himself, but couldn't. Tapping on each bag, he commented that one seemed empty but the other didn't. (So *what!*) To him, that seemed suspicious, and he again demanded that I open the "full" bag. I refused.

By this time, two other HP units had responded—who knows what the first HP claimed on the radio. He and another HP conferred *in my very presence* about coming up with some pretext to impound the bike so they could search it. My attitude grew quite hostile at that point and I snidely quipped that, *"You two were born about fifty years too late—the Führer could have used a couple of more guys like you!"* (Not recommended . . .)

Things *really* went downhill at that, and the third HP (a fairly reasonable guy, as it turned out) interceded, *"You have a really poor attitude! Have you had bad experiences with the police?"* He seemed genuinely concerned, so I replied, *"No, but I'm having one right now with him!"* (pointing to the HP who stopped me). *"Unless you can talk some sense into him, he's going to make a career mistake here and drag you two guys down with him."* That had the desired effect, so Nice HP took the first HP behind his car and calmed him down.

He returned, handed me my ticket, and the other guys drove off. While putting my gear back on, he honked and motioned me back to his car. *"Uh, oh,"* I mused; he's going to get me back there and concoct some story about me attacking him or something—anything to arrest me and impound the bike. *Very* warily, I approached his passenger window. He told me to get in and I understandably refused. He realized why I was suspicious and explained that he had made a mistake on my ticket. (HPs often cover several jurisdictions, and he had written the wrong court on my ticket.) He merely wanted to correct it, so I allowed him to do so, and he drove off.

Still smelling a rat, that he was trying send me to the *wrong* court (the "corrected" one), I sent Not Guilty pleas to *both* courts with an explanation. Happily, the HP's ticket somehow got *lost* between courts and nobody ever contacted me! *Heh!*

"Would you mind if I searched your...?"

Cops routinely ask to search, even when they really aren't all that suspicious. They know that it never hurts to ask. In fact, they are now trained to do so, for it bolsters their case if PC is later found insufficient. Don't get all weak-kneed if this happens to you. Use some verbal judo:

You: (Flat:) *"What would you be searching for?"*
Cop: *"Well, drugs."* (Sometimes it's for guns.)
You: (Cool:) *"Why didn't you first ask me if I had any in my car?"*

This politely shames the cop, and makes him look coarse and illmannered. Nobody ever speaks to cops this way, especially criminals. The cop will be knocked off track and likely become flustered over his embarrassment. He'll now get tougher:

Cop: (Impatient:) *"Well, if you've nothing to hide you shouldn't object to a search, should you?"*
You: (Light:) *"What a tired fig leaf that old line is! Then you wouldn't mind if I came over to your house and rummaged around, would you?"*
Cop: (Angry:) *"So, you're refusing to cooperate?"*
You: (Patient:) *"I neither participate in my own inconvenience, nor facilitate in wasting of taxpayer dollars by agreeing to time-consuming searches which can turn up nothing. There are criminals out there to be caught, and I suggest that you go find them or else your chief will read about this little scene in the newspapers tomorrow. If you really had probable cause you could have searched by now, without my consent. Since you obviously don't have it, I shall be on my way before you jeopardize your career any further."*

Criminals don't talk this way to the police. The cop will realize that you're the wrong guy to push about, and will make as face-saving retreat as he can. Granted, this kind of talk takes courage, but it's occasionally necessary.

Let me know how it goes!

TRAFFIC TICKETS

The only chance you'll have to talk your way out of a ticket entirely is to do it *before* he sets pen to pad. His tickets are precious revenue tools of the State, and he must account for each one. The odds of him ripping up a ticket are about the same as you putting Super Unleaded in a rental Yugo. You'll have only the first minute (or less) to talk your way out, as the cop must quickly decide whether or not to ticket you.

Many cops have the same lecturing attitude as third-grade teachers, so let them posture if it saves you a ticket. Allow the cop his spiel. No posterior kissing is necessary here, just play along with his scenario because it's to *your* advantage.

Some DON'Ts: *Don't* challenge, *don't* beg, *don't* threaten, *don't* cry, *don't* argue, *don't* get sarcastic, *don't* insin-uate that the cop is lying or prejudiced, *don't* lie about some "emergency," *don't* rationalize, *don't* whine, *don't* name drop.

David W. Kelly's *How To Talk Your Way Out Of A Traffic Ticket* (ISBN 0-918259-21-5) offers some good lines:

"I'm normally a safe driver, Officer, but for a second my at-tention was elsewhere. I promise I'll try to be more careful."

"Insurance for a person my age is quite high, so I have been trying to keep my record clean. Could you trust me to not make the same mistake again?"

"I have a perfect driving record. If you just give me a warn-ing this time, I'll do my best to keep it that way."

"I didn't realize that was illegal. I wouldn't have done it if I had known. I certainly know now!"

"I know this situation is my own fault. Can you excuse me this time? I promise you won't have to stop me again."

"It has been a long drive. You just made me realize I need to stop and get some coffee."

"I'm new to this area, Officer. I guess I need to pay closer attention to my driving."

It didn't work—he's writing you up

What you *might* be able to do is plead for a non-moving violation instead of a "mover." The State still gets its cash (which is all the State *really* cares about) but your record will not be affected by a ticket for a broken headlight, etc. In my experience, you'll have a 1 in 4 chance of this, and you must go for it before he reaches the violation line on your ticket. Try it!

Don't make it worse

Whatever the infraction, don't buy into a worse scene with a counterproductive attitude. Getting a ticket is bad enough. Keep the Scene at that level. *Never* tell the cop that you even *might* dispute a ticket, or he might tack on additional infractions. **Get your ticket and *go*.** (I ask the cop how to send in payment, for I want him to *believe* he's "made a "sale." He'll write fewer notes on the stop because of my apparent uninterest in disputing it.)

Save your "big guns" for the arraignment and trial, where you'll have the presumption of innocence in one of their over-loaded courts. *There* is where your advantage will be.

Making the ticket go away

You can either plead Not-Guilty and win in court (prefer-ably in a *jury* trial), or the State will drop the case (through De-fensive Driving Course, deferred adjudication, or a decline of prosecution). Of my contested tickets, the State dropped 1 in 3.

States vary in how serious they take your 5th and 6th Amendment rights for such offenses. Some states still allow a trial by jury (of usually 6). Most do not, and you will have a court trial before a judge (who will not appreciate his time being "wasted" on such puny matters).

Whichever, trial by jury or court, go whole hog. Demand a Bill of Particulars (a means of discovery enabling you to prepare a defense with less chance of being ambushed). Subpoena the repair records of the radar unit and the officer's training his-tory. Demand a court stenographer present. The DA may just decide it isn't worth his trouble. Happened often to me!

❖ 15

YOUR HOUSE & JOB

Inside your house (and business, if nonpublic and unregulated) you have the most rights. There is no intermediate level of intrusion such as the **Terry** frisk. And, if arrested inside, there is no inventory search of the room (although a search incident to arrest still applies to areas within *"grabbable distance."*)

The only legal way for the cops to come through your door *without* an exigency or your consent (both covered in Chapter 8 and assumed to be moot possibilities in your case) is via **arrest** already in progress from a public place, or a **warrant** (search or arrest). This chapter covers only those two avenues.

In view of that, coupled with the assumption that you are not a criminal, the chances of the police barging through your door are nearly nonexistent. There is, however, still the chance that someday the police will at least come to your house for questioning, and I'll show you how to handle that, too.

YOUR *"REASONABLE EXPECTATION OF PRIVACY"* WITHIN YOUR HOUSE

The 4th Amendment specifically protects your *"house"* from unwarranted police intrusions. The *"curtilage"* (or *"premises"*) around your house usually includes your garage/carport, a fenced-in backyard, and nearby buildings. Within your house and surrounding premises, you have a *"reasonable expectation of privacy."*

Such 4th Amendment protection does *not* extend to the *"open fields"* around your *"premises/curtilage,"* nor to front yards, porches, driveways, or sidewalks.

Anything that can be seen/heard/smelled by a passerby (mailman, neighbor, salesman, etc.) without any extra effort is fair game for probable cause—though, a warrant is still necessary to gain entry.

"KNOCK, KNOCK — *POLICE!*"

If the police come to your door to question you, *beware.* It's for *their* benefit, not yours. As I explained in Chapter 5, there is rarely any advantage to speaking with the police about your affairs. Help them catch criminals, but don't talk about yourself.

If you have information about a crime, either speak to them *through* a closed door (not window), or over the phone. Use a speaker or intercom. **Never allow them in your house.** While they may insist, cajole, or even plead, *keep them outside*—one way or another. If such strikes them as suspicious, explain that the house is not tidied up for guests, or that everybody has the flu. Do *not* budge on this! You have control of the contact, not them. Keep them outside.

There is a great scene in my *Molôn Labé!* on this very point if you need a dramatic example of precisely how to handle a doorstep field interview. (pp. 203-5)

If you've reported an incident in your house and the police are there to investigate, make sure you've locked up all irrelevant areas and sensitive items (guns, papers, cash, etc.). If the entire house seems within investigative scope, lock up the stuff in your car (parked in your driveway, not on the street). Do not allow them to wander about unaccompanied. When their job is done, politely escort them out. Be cordial, but not overly friendly. Remember, they don't work for you, they work for the *State*—and you know what the State is in search of . . .

HOW TO ARREST IN A HOUSE

The Suspect's House

No amount of PC, even 100% certainty that the evidence or "wanted" person is inside, will justify a warrantless entry. (Not *yet*, anyway . . .)

A warrant is necessary only if the subject or evidence is *already inside* the house/curtilage. If the cops have PC (though no warrant) to arrest you, and they see you in your front yard, on your porch, or even inside your house behind the front door cracked open—they may proceed to come inside your house since the arrest began in a "public" place. As ruled in ***U.S. v. Santana***, 427 US 38, 42-43 (1976), *"a suspect may not defeat an arrest which has been set in motion in a public place by...the expedient of escaping to a private place."*

Practical tips

If you believe the police have PC (though not yet a warrant) to arrest, stay in your house, and do not open the door. Draw all curtains. Do *not* answer the door or phone, as such will give the cops PC to believe that you're inside.

If you believe that a warrant *is* imminent, then you obviously do *not* want to be arrested *inside* your house. Stay outside your house and car. If you are picked up, you want it to occur as a pedestrian in public. You want to keep the police outside your property, if possible. (If, however, they have a *search* warrant, then tough—the police *will* gain lawful entry.)

Unless you want to hide out, perhaps the best thing to do is voluntarily appear with your lawyer. Such will look very good to the court and DA, save yourself a lot of pre-arrest worry, *and* possibly keep the police out of your house.

For those, however, who cannot bring themselves to simply give up to the police, yet cannot stay in their house, one solid option exists: leave the jurisdiction and hole up in a hotel (paid with cash), or a third party's house. I mention this, not to assist real criminals, but to assist those who might become victim to a baseless or politically-motivated action. The government's hands are rarely clean, and one might someday fall under undue persecution.

A third party's house

In order to enter a third party's house (where the arrestee is not domiciled) a cop must have a *search* warrant (unless consent or exigency is present) according to **Steagald v. United States**, 451 US 204 (1981). Assuming there's no PC to search the third party's house, the police cannot obtain a search warrant as a pretext to arrest a subject.

Make sure this friend will not give you up, and has a cool, unflappable demeanor. Do not use his phone or expose yourself to view. Do not tell *anybody* of your location—not even your lawyer, unless he assures you of an attorney-client relationship and his mandated silence. Even then, I'd hesitate revealing your location, as his phone could be monitored.

WHEN THEY HAVE A WARRANT

Search Warrant only

The warrant should be specific and accurate. *"Premises"* is broader than *"house"* and they cannot search beyond the scope stated in the warrant. Try very hard to see and read the warrant yourself during (if not before) the search. If they have utterly the wrong address, tell them and firmly demand that they leave at once. If they refuse, demand immediate "judicial review" by the court. Refusal exhibits "bad faith" on their part and should nullify the warrant, if not get you some damages in a lawsuit.

You will not be arrested unless they find contraband. You and others *will,* however, be detained inside (**Michigan v. Summers**, 452 US 692 (1981)). Visitors who cannot be immediately tied to crime-related activity should not be detained further, much less arrested.

Try to camcord the search. Expect improper search procedures, abusive behavior (such as that BATF agent Donna Slusser stomping to death a family kitten), and even planted evidence. The cops will try to forbid the filming, but as long as you're not interfering with a lawful search, they have no legal right to stop you. Admit nothing—in fact, say nothing.

Arrest Warrant only

If the police knock and announce that they have an arrest warrant for you, reply that you are unarmed and are coming out. Empty all your pockets, and seek to leave through an unguarded exit, lock it behind you, and meet them with your hands held high. **You want them to arrest you *outside* your house, if possible.** Doing so will lessen your *"grabbable reach"* and thus the scope of the *"search incident to lawful arrest."* Wherever they first see you, that's where they get to search. The best place for them to arrest you is in your backyard, which is semiprivate, yet outside.

They might have the back door covered, so pick another exit without making it look like you're trying to flee. If you open the front door, they will enter and arrest you inside. So, think in advance of the optimum exit. In the foyer, or kitchen back door is probably best.

If arrested *inside,* the police can usually make a *"protective sweep"* of the entire premises (not just *"grabbable reach"*) to search for dangerous persons. During such a sweep, they cannot search in places incapable of concealing a person, such as small containers. These sweeps are also much harder to justify if the arrest takes place outside, though not impossible.

Both Search *and* Arrest Warrants

You got problems. First, you will be arrested, and second, they get to ransack your house. You'll have no freedom to camcord the search, or even tape-record the arrest (though others present might).

No-Knock Warrants

Usually the police must knock-announce-wait during the execution of a warrant. The exceptions to this requirement are:

❑ The warrant expressly authorizes forcible entry without prior announcement. The cop's affidavit must state specific, explainable reasons why he cannot knock and announce, or,

❑ Circumstances known to the cop *after* the warrant's issue give him PC to believe that notice prior entry is likely:

❶   to result in the easy destruction/disposal of evidence; or
❷   to endanger one's life or safety; or
❸   to enable the suspect to escape; or
❹   a "useless gesture" as those inside know why the police are there and will not respond, or the police *know* no one is inside.

Allegedly, it is very difficult for the cops to convince a court *ex post facto* that these exceptional difficulties existed. "Best" yet, even if they are required to knock and announce, they have to wait only a *"reasonable"* amount of time before entering if the dweller delays or refuses to answer the door. What is a *"reasonable"* time length? ***U.S. v. Cruz***, 265 F.Supp 15, 23-24 (W.D. Tex. 1967) ruled **15 seconds!** Great.

AH, SWEET PRIVACY!

In my case, there is not a scrap of paper to link me to my house. I have no phone, utility, rent, or mortgage records in my name. No license, credit card, or bill has my house location on it. *Nada.* In today's atmosphere, full of snoops, nosy do-gooders, bloodthirsty collection agencies, litigious leeches, and an increasingly militarized police, it makes no sense to be easily located.

While I realize that this sounds "paranoid" to most of you, think of the advantages: your assets are generally safe from lawsuits, credit hounds cannot bang at your door, you can't be arrested in your pajamas for some old speeding ticket, "old friends" cannot drop by because they "just happened to be in the neighborhood," old romances cannot disturb you, etc.

Such is easy to arrange, too. Using a street addressed (not a P.O. Box) mail receiving service ("A") as your "home address" you can then rent/own a domicile elsewhere (preferably in another name). The mail drop, which unknowingly has *another* mail drop address ("B") as your "real" address (and vice-versa) receives all your mail and bills. Your real home is free of all that and the related headaches. Your public phone number is merely a voice mail, while your home phone is established in another name.

I have lived like this for many years. The catalyst for all this was nearly being arrested at my doorstep for an old speeding ticket (which had been paid, but the record lost by computer). Though eventually sorted out, I resolved never to allow such to happen again.

Years later, because of these prior arrangements, I easily avoided being subpoenaed for an utterly baseless $800 civil suit filed by a money-grubbing pest (and full-time cretin). The paper-serving deputy simply couldn't find me, so the pest had no choice but to glomm onto somebody else.

I also avoided the constant nuisance of a remarkably unbalanced woman who, being desperately unhappy with her marriage, developed an unprovoked fixation on me (a platonic friend), almost to the point of a "fatal attraction." She was quite ingenious and persistent in her efforts to find me, going to such lengths as to even call my family impersonating credit card representatives and hospital staff. While she fooled a few people and managed to wheedle bits of information, she never found out where I lived or worked. After months of trying, she finally gave up and became fixated on someone else.

Finally, these arrangements have allowed me, pseudo-nymously, to write material critical of oppressive government and helpful to liberty-minded folks. While *anybody* can be located with enough time and expense, I am simply not *worth* such effort—which is fine by me.

I yearn for a polite and respectful world where I could have a listed phone number in my own name without concern of being bothered, but it ain't gonna happen any time soon. Even though I'm a dreamer and an optimist, I'm a realist, *first*. Privacy is like fire insurance; you can't get it *after* you need it. You get it first, and then hope that it never becomes necessary.

My book *Bulletproof Privacy* will explain most of what any of you need to know.

CHECKPOINT DRUG DOGS

Pardon this out-of-chapter inclusion, but the Supreme Court just allowed (1/2005) drug dogs during suspicionless checkpoint stops. (Plain smell, you know.) But, no worries; you've got Boston on your side. My countermeasure? Make the dog *terrified* of your car. How? With the **Dazer** from U.S. Cavalry (888-888-7228; stock #N9539; $34.95 plus $7.95 s&h). Other mail-order companies carry such devices, so test them.

> [This ultrasonic dog deterrent is a] *high-tech alternative to chemical sprays or physical violence. A 2-3 second burst or quick on/off action deliver a discomforting yet humane, high-frequency sound inaudible to humans.* ***Aggressive dogs become dazed or confused and retreat to a safe distance. Effective up to 15' away.*** *Includes a long-life 9V battery. Measures 2"x4½". 3 ozs.*

A foolproof way for the cops to create probable cause (PC) is to have a drug-sniffing dog "alert" to drug scent by touching a twig of pot in his pocket and wiping the scent on your car. It's guaranteed PC on demand. I know; it happened to *me.*

During a stop you will not be able to hold the Dazer. So, mount it in your car. To hardwire it, buy a 12V to 9V power jack for cigarette lighters (KMart, Radio Shack, etc. sell them for $8. Keep the 9V battery as backup). I'd replace the Dazer's internal switch with a switch/oscillating relay hidden under your dash or in your glovebox. (The oscillation turns the Dazer rapidly on and off for best effect.) The Dazer itself (or at least its speaker) should be mounted under the car, probably pointing at the ground. (Left inside the car it might not be loud enough.)

I'd also activate the Dazer whenever you are on the public roads or parking lots. That way, your car is protected while you're inside a store, etc. (And you might not have the opportunity during a traffic stop if detained outside your car.)

Checkpoint or traffic stop, the drug dog is neutralized. He won't get *near* your car. In fact, he'll want only to run to the squad car and cower on the back seat. The cops will be extremely baffled and disturbed by this. **No sniff, no alert, no PC, *no search.*** Freedom through superior technology!

Do *try* to keep a straight face. Have a Great Daze(r).

YOU & YOUR GUNS

IS THE 2nd AMENDMENT AN INDIVIDUAL OR COLLECTIVE RIGHT?

A well-regulated militia, being necessary to the security of a free state, the right of the people to keep and bear arms shall not be infringed.
    — Second Amendment to the Constitution

[Textual exegesis] *suggests that "the people" protected by the Fourth Amendment, and by the First **and Second** Amendments, and to whom rights and powers are reserved under the Ninth and Tenth Amendments, refers to a class of persons who are part of a national community or who have developed sufficient connection with this country to be considered part of that community.*
    — *U.S. v. Verdugo-Urquidez,* 494 US 259,265 (1990)

It would . . . be strange to find in the midst of a catalog of the rights of individuals a provision securing to the states the right to maintain a designated "Militia." **Dispassionate scholarship suggests quite strongly that the right of the people to keep and bear arms meant just that.** *There is no need to deceive ourselves as to what the Second Amendment said and meant.*
    — Justice Antonin Scalia, *A Matter of Interpretation: Federal Courts and the Law* (Princeton University Press)

This Court has not had (i.e., more like "chosen") *recent occasion to consider the nature of the substantive right safeguarded by the Second Amendment. If, however, the Second Amendment is read to confer a personal right to "keep and bear arms," a colorable argument exists that the Federal Government's regulatory scheme, at*

least as it pertains to the purely intrastate sale or possession of firearms, runs afoul of that Amendment's protections.
— *Printz v. U.S.,* 521 US 898, 937-938 & n.1,2 (1997)
(Thomas, J., concurring)

As languidly as the 2nd Amendment was written, the *"People"* of the 2nd are the same *"People"* as in the 1st, 4th, 9th, and 10th. Any intellectually honest scholar must agree.

The tired and feeble argument that the 2nd meant only the National Guards is absurd, as such did not even exist until over a century after the Bill of Rights had been written.

What has the Supreme Court been doing?

As an indisputable constitutional bulwark, you'd think the Court would have been upholding the 2nd Amendment all this time. *Au contraire!* Don't look to the Court to strike down modern gun control legislation. They've denied *certiorari* every time since 1939:

I cannot help but suspect that the best explanation for the absence of the Second Amendment from the legal consciousness of the elite bar, including that component found in the legal academy, is derived from a mixture of sheer opposition to the idea of private ownership of guns and the perhaps subconscious fear that altogether plausible, perhaps even "winning," interpretations of the Second Amendment would present real hurdles to those of us supporting prohibitory regulation. . . . [T]he Amendment may be profoundly embarrassing to many who both support such regulation and view themselves as committed to zealous adherence to the Bill of Rights (such as most members of the ACLU).
— Stanford Levinson, *The Embarrassing Second Amendment,*
sourced from *Safeguarding Liberty*

Meanwhile, become educated. Visit www.atf.treas.gov/core. The best digest is *Gun Laws of America* by Alan Korwin (www.bloomfieldpress.com). It covers *all* federal gun laws, and although I resent the fact that I must pay $20 for a book on federal gun laws (because there shouldn't *be* any), this book is a must. The summaries alone are invaluable. The novel *Unintended Consequences* by John Ross also contains excellent narratives on gun control laws. In this chapter (all lifted from my *Boston's Gun Bible*) I'll cover the main laws which affect us generally. For wider or deeper detail, you'll have to dive in yourself.

NATIONAL FIREARMS ACT of 1934

Until 1933, you could order a new .45 Thompson subma-chinegun from the Sears catalog for $125, *with leather case.* You could own a BAR or an M1919A4. Silencers (or, more accu-rately, gun *mufflers*) were sold at the hardware store for under $5. You could even have $20 gold pieces in your pocket. What a great time to be a gunowner!

Since Prohibition had been repealed by the 22nd Amend-ment in 1933, thousands of Treasury agents were idle by 1934 and, golly, they needed *some* kind of work. So, create a new class of criminals. (What else is new?)

The *NFA34* was our first serious federal gun law. Unless you have paid a $200 Treasury tax stamp, you cannot legally own an automatic weapon, silencer, or any long gun less than 26" overall or with a barrel less than 18" (this was amended to 16" for rifles in 1958). Privately-owned gold had been generally restricted just one year earlier. (Good thing that alcohol had been decriminalized—*I'd* sure want a drink after Congress passed the *National Banking Act* and *National Firearms Act!*)

Not generally known is that the *original* language would have included *all handguns*, but women made such a proper and righteous stink that the handgun inclusion was stricken.

The phony rationale for *NFA34*

It was the Valentine's Day Massacre of 1929 and other similar gangster machinegunnings, but these infrequent inci-dents had all but ceased with Prohibition's end a year earlier. As Vin Suprynowicz rhetorically asked in his *Send In The Waco Killers*, why don't beer distributors today gun each other down?

So, what was the *real* reason?

The National Firearms Act fit in perfectly with the systematic creation of government programs and deficit spending that Franklin Roo-sevelt immediately began to institute the instant he took office. The NFA was a model vehicle for the continued expansion of govern-ment power: It was arbitrary (i.e., the 18-inch rule); it gave the gov-ernment sweeping authority over something very common; it focused on inanimate objects rather than criminal behavior; it levied draconian taxes on these objects; and most certainly, it created mil-lions of criminals with the stroke of a pen, just as Prohibition had.

— John Ross, *Unintended Consequences* (1996), p. 356

There are nearly 200,000 *NFA34* weapons on record. Only *two* have ever been used (both by cops!) to commit a crime. Nevertheless, the feds will eventually try to confiscate these weapons *without compensation* just as they did in 1994 with the Striker and Street Sweeper shotguns.

GUN CONTROL ACT of 1968

*The Congress hereby declares that the purpose of this title is to provide support for Federal, State, and local law enforcement officials in their fight against crime and violence, **and it is not the purpose of this title to place any undue or unnecessary Federal restrictions or burdens on law-abiding citizens** with respect to the acquisition, possession, or use of firearms appropriate to the purpose of hunting, trapshooting, targetshooting, personal protection, or other lawful activity, **and that this title is not intended to discourage or eliminate the private ownership or use of firearms by law-abiding citizens for lawful purposes**, or provide for the imposition by Federal regulations of any procedures or requirements other than those reasonably necessary to implement and effectuate the provisions of this title.*

— *Gun Control Act of 1968* preamble

Bullsh✳t. *Unbelievable* bullsh✳t. This preamble reminds me of the FBI at Waco on 19 April 1993 shouting through their tanks' bullhorns *"This is not an assault!"* (The Davidians should have fired back, shouting, *"These are not bullets!"*)

In 1968, Senator Dodd remembered Hitler's 1938 gun control legislation from the Nuremberg trials and requested its translation for his study. Just a few months later Congress passed a virtual clone of Hitler's gun registration scheme (designed to prohibit guns to Jews and other minorities). Chillingly, the Nazi *"sporting purpose"* rationale was used in *GCA68*. Aaron Zelman's "Jews For The Preservation of Firearm Ownership" (www.jpfo.org) proved this in their *Gateway To Tyranny* with its side-by-side comparison of both laws.

Zelman sent a copy of *Gateway* to every Congressman, Senator, and Supreme Court Justice, and to all the media. Silence. Not even the *conservative* and *libertarian* press dared to touch this bombshell. First, Nazi-style gun regulation. Then, the camps. In 1998 there were guys in Montana welding shackles to the insides of railroad boxcars. (I spoke to the brother of one the welders, so this isn't rumor.) Folks, do the math.

Using the *"interstate/foreign commerce"* clause for the second time in gun regulation, *GCA68* prohibited the mail-order receipt of firearms, the importation of foreign weapons *"unsuitable for sporting purposes,"* and the ownership of unregistered *"destructive devices"* (*e.g.*, mortars, bazookas, smokeless powder weapons with a bore in excess of ½").

It mandated the BATF Form 4473 and prohibited the sale of firearms and ammunition to certain *"prohibited persons."*

The phony rationale for *GCA68*
The murders of JFK, RFK, and MLK.

So, what was the *real* reason?
To create the foundation of a national firearm registry, the means to a confiscation end.

18 USC §922(d) *"prohibited possessors"*
(d) it shall be unlawful for any person to sell or otherwise dispose of any firearm or ammunition to any person knowing or having reasonable cause to believe that such person—
(1) is under indictment for, or has been convicted in any court of, a crime punishable by imprisonment for a term exceeding one year;
(2) is a fugitive from justice (BTP note: This means, according to §921(15), having *"fled any State to avoid prosecution for a crime or to avoid giving testimony in any criminal proceeding."*—so remaining in hiding within your State is OK?);
(3) is an unlawful user of or addicted to any controlled substance (as defined in section 102 of the Controlled Substances Act (21 U.S.C. 802));
(4) has been adjudicated as a mental defective or has been committed to any mental institution (political dissidents beware of Soviet-style psychiatric sentences);
(5) who, being an alien, is illegally or unlawfully in the United States;
(6) who has been discharged from the Armed Forces under dishonorable conditions;
(7) who, having, been a citizen of the United States, has renounced his citizenship (word your untaxation and rescission affidavits very carefully), *or;*
(8) is subject to a court order that restrains such person from harassing, stalking, or threatening an intimate partner of such person or child of such intimate partner or person, or engaging in other conduct that would place an intimate partner in reasonable fear of bodily

injury to the partner or child, except that this paragraph shall only apply to a court order that—

(A) was issued after a hearing of which such person received actual notice, and at which such person had the opportunity to participate; and

(B)(i) includes a finding that such person represents a credible threat to the physical safety of such intimate partner or child; or

(ii) by its terms explicitly prohibits the use, attempted use, or threatened use of physical force against such intimate partner or child that would reasonably be expected to cause bodily injury.

The "Lautenberg Amendment"

§658 was snuck in the 1997 *Department of Defense Appropriations Act.* This ugly bit added to the *"prohibited possessor"* list anybody convicted of a **misdemeanor** *"crime of domestic violence"* involving the use or attempted use of physical force, or the threatened use of a deadly weapon, among family members (spouse, parent, guardian, cohabitor, or similar). Spouses slapping each other, or spanking their child, can be such a *"crime."* I'm not making light of actual wife *battering*, but to ban somebody from owning guns because they threw a cereal bowl at their spouse is going to ridiculous extremes.

***Never* before has a *misdemeanor* offense, and an *ex post facto* one at that, been grounds for denial of the constitutional right to own and carry guns.** According to Alan Korwin, *"It is as if a former speeding ticket were now grounds for felony arrest if you own a car or gasoline."* It denies *"due process"* (felony accountability without Grand Jury indictment; dispossession of lawful private property without *"just compensation"*; equal protection of the law, right to accusation, counsel, trial, and jury; among many others).

18 USC § 922(g)(8) struck down in Federal Court

This subsection forbade those under domestic restraining orders from owning a gun, was struck down by a US District judge on 2nd Amendment grounds:

It is absurd that a boilerplate state court divorce order can collaterally and automatically extinguish a law-abiding citizen's Second Amendment rights, particularly when neither the judge issuing the order, nor the parties nor their attorneys are aware of the federal criminal penalties arising from firearm possession after entry of the restraining order. That such a routine civil order has such extensive consequences totally attenuated from divorce proceedings makes the statute unconstitutional. There must be a limit to government

> *regulation on lawful firearm possession. This statute exceeds that limit, and therefore is unconstitutional.*

. . . and on 5th Amendment grounds:

> [Since the statute is an] *obscure, highly technical statute with no mens rea requirement, it violates Emerson's Fifth Amendment due process rights subject to prosecution without proof of knowledge that he was violating the statute.*
>> — *U.S. v. Emerson,* Northern District of Texas, San Angelo
>> 7 April 1999

Judge Sam R. Cummings deserves our respect and praise for his fine ruling. (The 5th Circuit later held that the 2nd Amendment protects an *individual* right to keep and bear arms, although such could be regulated in certain cases. Look up the case on www.sas-aim.org or www.gunowners.org.)

THE "BRADY BILL"

Signed into law on 30 November 1993 and found at 18 USC §922(s&t), *The Brady Handgun Violence Prevention Act* mandated (for states without an instant-check system) waiting-period provisions for dealer handgun purchases after 28 February 1994. (These expired on 27 February 1999.) It contains extremely tortuous language. One sentence has *532* words.

Brady attempted to require the states to enforce Federal law at the states' expense, and the Supreme Court struck this portion of *Brady* down 5-4 on 27 June 1997 (***Printz v. U.S.***) as an improper use of the *"interstate commerce"* regulatory power. This is no real setback for the feds, as their *National Instant Criminal Background Check* (NICBC) system has been up since 30 November 1998. (This NICBC will predictably auger in a national ID with biometric numbering of your thumbprint.)

The phony rationale of "Brady"

The attempted assassination by John Hinckley, Jr. of President Reagan, and the wounding of James Brady.

So, what's the *real* reason?

To infringe more on your 2nd Amendment rights.

Changing from NICBC to NICS

The law named the check system the *"national instant criminal background check"* system (NICBC), but the feds are now calling it the National Instant Check System (NICS, rhymes with "nix" which I find illuminating). Notice how they've eliminated *"criminal background"* from the name? They did this so that the system can be later *expanded* to a system of withholding *permission* for reasons *other* than an applicant's criminal background. (Talk about getting "nixed.") Such could be suspected (not convicted) *"crimes"* of tax evasion, *"money laundering,"* or even political dissention. Just you wait, NICS will prove to be the camel's nose under the tent.

LAWS ON *"ASSAULT WEAPONS"*
18 USC §922(r)

*It shall be unlawful for any person to assemble **from imported parts** any semiautomatic rifle or shotgun which is identical to any rifle or shotgun prohibited from importation under section 925(d)(3) of this chapter as **not being particularly suitable for or readily adaptable to sporting purposes** . . .*

It is because of this that post-11/90 mag-fed foreign semi-autos must have that "sporter" stock. §925(d)(3) long guns are 26 USC §5845(a) *1934 NFA* weapons (machineguns, <18"bbl shotguns, etc.) and surplus military firearms. Non-*NFA* and non-military firearms which are *"particularly suitable for or readily adaptable to sporting purposes"* may be customized.

"GUN-FREE SCHOOL ZONES"

The Florida tourist-shooting epidemic is also relevant in another way. Once the airport rental lots started removing their big fluorescent rent-a-car stickers, Florida's "tourist-murder crime wave" disappeared virtually overnight. (Because criminals rightly figured that out-of-town tourists weren't armed like the Floridians were.) Similarly, one of the last places a criminal knows he can find unarmed victims in an increasingly well-armed and peaceful America today . . . is in the "gun-free school zones" in which the snivelliberals have locked up our children. (BTP Note: The correlation between school zone gun bans and school shootings is far too high to be ignored. Somebody should figure the "r" value on this.)

— Vin Suprynowicz, *Send in the Waco Killers* (1999), p. 384

The *Gun-Free School Zones Act of 1991* (which was found at 18 USC §922(q)) prohibited the knowing possession of a firearm on or within 1,000 feet of a school. America had 121,855 schools as of 1994, and their 1,000' zones covered just about anywhere a gunowner would typically drive or travel. This was no accident. It's already illegal in every State to use a gun reck-lessly *on* school property, so Congress *didn't* have children's safety in mind. Since concealed-carry permit holders were ex-empted, it was an obvious ploy to herd all the other gunowners into the artificial CHL corral (eventually to be eliminated).

In *Hologram of Liberty* I thoroughly covered the Supreme Court's reversal (1995 *U.S. v. Lopez*) of this act. Undeterred, Congress simply repassed the struck down act in §657 of the 2,000 page DoD Appropriations Act of 1997. Congressmen voted for this Act without even having read the thing. Typical.

The only difference in this new version is that the phrase *"that has moved in or that otherwise affects interstate or foreign commerce"* was added in two places. Since this new language alone would not seem to affect the Supreme Court's *Lopez* 5-4 decision, I suspect that Rehnquist and/or O'Connor have been privately dealt with and that a 5-4 or 6-3 reversal of *Lopez* can be expected. Even if the 5 Justice *Lopez* majority holds fast, Congress will nevertheless enjoy 2-4 years of "free" enforce-ment and many innocent people will become convicted felons.

The *"Self-defense Free Zones"*

The Clinton-era rash of school shootings was, in a way, predictable. Peaceable folks are forbidden to be armed on school property, and the murderous maniacs have taken notice. (Israel used to suffer from terrorist attacks on her schools and airliners, until Israel got wise and began to arm teachers and pi-lots. The attacks quickly stopped.) In Texas, which passed its CHL in 1996, guns are banned from several types of establishments, including churches, sports arenas, government offices, courts, airports and restaurants serving alcohol.

I wanted to know why the state treats teachers like second-class citizens, when plumbers and doctors are allowed to protect themselves on the job. I would be happier sending my child to a school where a teacher whom I trust is armed and well prepared.
  We have created a shopping list for madmen. *If guns are the problem, why don't we see things occurring at skeet and trap shoots, at gun shows, at NRA conventions?* ***We only see it where***

guns aren't allowed. The sign of a gun with a slash through it is like a neon sign for gunmen—'We're unarmed. Come kill us.'
— Texas Representative Suzanna Gratia Hupp

Hupp's point was utterly proven on 9/11 when 19 terrorists armed with boxcutters took over and destroyed four airliners.

SO, WHAT RIGHTS ARE *LEFT?*

Not many, but it could be much, much worse.

You may ship a long gun *intrastate* through the mails
Send it by registered mail with no outside "gun" markings. Handguns cannot be mailed, but must be sent by common carrier such as FedEx, RPS, UPS, etc.

You may ship interstate to *yourself* in care of the recipient
If shipping to yourself out of state, address it to yourself c/o the recipient (who cannot open the box). This can be useful if you don't want to chance losing a gun in a checked airline bag.

You may buy ammo privately (preferably at a gun show)
Until 1986, you had to fill out a form to buy ammo, but no longer. You can even order the stuff by the case from out of State and have it sent right to your door (although I'd order it under an alias and receive it at a Mail Boxes Etc. for Ø3). Stock up *now* on affordable, quality, anonymous ammo—while we can.

Transfer intrastate firearms privately, without an FFL
The feds do not yet regulate the private, *intra*state transfer between nonlicensed adults. As long as the buyer or recipient is not an 18 USC §922(d) *"prohibited possessor" and* the nonlicensed transfer is legal in your home state and city, you may privately buy/sell used firearms as you can used books or clothing. You may buy/sell from classified ads, garage sales, flea markets, gun shows, etc.
The other party must be from your home state, to avoid the applicability of *"interstate commerce"* federal gun laws.
Do not expect this right to last much longer. The gun haters are beside themselves that in 23 States no record of sale is required to be reported to the State or local government. (These states are: Alaska, Arizona, Arkansas, Colorado,

Delaware, Florida, Georgia, Idaho, Kansas, Kentucky, Louisiana, Maine, Mississippi, Montana, Nebraska, Nevada, New Mexico, Oklahoma, Texas, Utah, Vermont, West Virginia, and Wyoming.) Since most of these states will *never* ban record-free private sales, the feds will try to, some day.

Out-of-State transfer through a bequest

You'll need to go through a local FFL and fill out a BATF Form 4473 to legally send or receive (even as gifts) firearms from out-of-state. The only exception to this is a bequest.

A temporary loan or rental of a firearm for lawful sporting purposes can be made interstate.

Interstate shipment of firearms for repair, etc.

You may send *and receive* a firearm through a common carrier (*e.g.*, FedEx, RPS, UPS, etc.) to a repair facility directly from your home without an FFL intermediary. When sending to a non-FFL, you must declare in writing to the common carrier that you are sending a firearm.

Interstate transportation of firearms

The NRA has a good pamphlet on this. *Generally*, if your gun is legal at your destination, then you may carry it *unloaded, cased, and locked in the trunk* of your car.

Many states (MA, NY, NJ, CA, etc.) are quirky about this with handguns and semiautomatic rifles. *Beware.*

You may take an unloaded/cased/locked/declared gun in your checked-through airline baggage. The airline may *not* place on your bag any identifying "steal me!" gun tag, but they *will* code the tag, usually with an "FFFFFFFFFFF."

Open carry of firearms

Only 28 states allow this. States in **bold** also allow the unrecorded private transfers of firearms. States *italicized* have strong preemptions against local infringement of gun rights:

Alabama, **Alaska, Arizona, Colorado, Delaware,** *Idaho,* **Kansas,** *Kentucky, Louisiana,* **Maine, Mississippi,** Missouri, **Montana, Nebraska, Nevada,** New Hampshire, Ohio, **Oklahoma,** Oregon, Pennsylvania, *New Mexico, North Carolina, South Dakota,* **Vermont,** Virginia, **West Virginia,** Wisconsin, and *Wyoming.*

Obviously, the best States here are Idaho, Kentucky, Louisiana, New Mexico, Vermont, and Wyoming.

Concealed carry of firearms

Some 34 states (check www.nra.org) have a *"shall issue"* concealed handgun license (CHL) system. (4 others have discretionary, though relaxed, systems which are considered *de facto "shall issue."*) Generally, as long as you're not a *"prohibited possessor"* and you take a safety training course, the State *must* approve your CHL permit application.

In a dozen or so states, the local police chief or sheriff has the arbitrary power of refusal (and they use it *frequently,* most infamously in Kalifornia).

In Illinois, Kansas, Nebraska, Ohio, Wisconsin, and DC. there is no provision for CHLs. *Zip. Nada. Keine.*

Only *Vermont* and *Alaska* perfectly recognize your right to be peaceably armed *without* permit—openly or concealed. So, Sarah Brady and Josh Sugarmann—why aren't *Vermont* and *Alaska* a hotbed of gun violence when they *should* be by your stupid argument?

Conversely, why is Washington, DC., where they've *banned* handgun ownership, our nation's *murder* capital? CHL states have lower crime rates. This is indisputable. Every Swiss male keeps at home his *fully-automatic,* militia-issued rifle (along with grenades, mortars, etc.), and Switzerland has the lowest crime rate of the West.

Look, Brady and Sugarmann, you clowns—opposing political views are one thing, but you don't have the *decency* to be intellectually *honest!* You are liars, creeps, and cowards. You pervert our language through your Orwellian, neurolinguistic programming in order to make us all defenseless against criminals and government thugs alike. *Jackals!*

HOW THE BATFE OPERATES

OK, now that you've read about federal gun laws and are now all riled up about their unconstitutional assault on your rights, it's now time to discuss your enemy, the BATFE.

Back in 2002 I wondered in *Boston's Gun Bible* how a Title 26 USC (*NFA34*) *tax*-collecting bureau within the Department of Treasury can legally enforce Title *18* USC criminal gun statutes (*e.g.,* the 1990 import ban and the 1994 *"Crime Bill"*). Apparently, they heard me and in January 2003 rolled the Treasury Bureau of Alcohol, Tobacco, and Firearms into the Department of Justice as the BATFE ("E" for explosives). This must really rankle former BATF agents already upset enough about not being a "cool" 3 letter agency (*i.e.*, FBI, DEA, NSA, etc.). Now they are a very uncool 5 letter bunch.

Most BATFE busts are based on stings and entrapments. BATmen won't scour the urban ghettos for *gangstas'* Uzis, but they *will* try to lure the uninformed and stupid into traps. It's not about fighting violent crime (which is dangerous work), but about hounding peaceable gunowners out of existence.

They can only bust three kinds of folks: the sellers, the buyers, and the owners. Regarding such busts, there's the to/from *whom*, the *what*, the *when*, the *where*, and the *how*.

spotting the BATFE agent(s) at gun shows

These people have *no* love for guns or their history, and it shows. They handle guns like they were soiled diapers. Usually working in pairs, they are often abrupt, impatient, and arrogant. Preoccupation with unknown matters (*i.e.,* they're calculating how to best bust you) can be a clue to their identity. If he initiates a dialogue (with you, a *stranger*) about illegal items or activities, then it's 90% sure that he's a fed.

If you suspect a buyer or seller to be an agent, ask if he is a local. If answers affirmatively, then ask to see his driver's license (ostensibly to verify his State residency). He will be quite reluctant to do this, for several reasons. One, cops and feds often keep their DL inside their badge case to smoothly identify themselves during traffic stops as brother officers (thus avoiding the ticket). Two, his DL *might* show his home address (though their office address is more likely). Third, he's used to demanding *other* people's DLs, not vice versa. (It'll rankle him.)

If the guy (or woman) still seems hinky, politely decline to transact. Then, have a friend follow him around the show, or even to his car.

The agent's car

Because of their arrogance and low mental wattage, these people are tactically sloppy. Count on his many mistakes. Look for cop paraphernalia in the car interior. Some clues are: radio mikes, windshield/dashboard notepads, law enforcement paperwork or magazines, handcuffs, batons, Maglites, etc.

External clues are: blackwall tires, A-pillar spotlights, roof/trunk lid telltale round spots in the dust where the magnetic antenna mount was, and a general cop presence.

Look at the rear license plate and its screw heads for evidence of frequent plate swapping (undercover feds have a trunkful of plates from many States). Get the dashboard VIN. If it's not a dedicated undercover vehicle with bogus registration, then running a "10-27" check might prove useful.

DO *NOT* BUY/SELL OUT-OF-STATE

Under federal law (based on interstate commerce clause regulations), you must be a resident of that State to directly transfer any firearm (even one bought or sold privately), else you'll fall within the *interstate* regulatory grasp of Title 18. From ATF Form 4473 (4-97) Definitions:

> 6. State of Residence - *The State in which an individual resides.* **An individual resides in a State if he or she is present in a State with the intention of making a home in that State.** *If an individual is on active duty as a member of the Armed Forces, the individual's State of residence is the State in which his or her permanent duty station is located. An alien who is legally in the United States shall be considered to be a resident in the State for a period of at least 90 days prior to the date of sale or delivery of a firearm. The following are examples that illustrate this definition:*

Example 1. A maintains a home in State X. A travels to State Y on a hunting, fishing, business, or other type of trip. A does not become a resident of State Y by reason of such trip.

Example 2. A is a U.S. citizen and maintains a home in State X and a home in State Y. A resides in State X except for weekends or the summer months of the year and in State Y for weekends or the summer months of the year. During the time that A actually resides in State X, A is a resident of State X, and during the time that A actually resides in State Y, A is a resident of State Y.

Example 3. A, an alien, travels on vacation or on a business trip to State X. Regardless of the length of the time A spends in State X, A does not have a State of residence in State X. This is because A does not have a home in State X at which he has resides for at least 90 days.

While I have *never* advocated committing crimes which are *mala in se* (*i.e.*, evil in themselves), freedom-loving Americans should routinely challenge all *mala prohibita* (wrongs, though not evil, yet prohibited). I can think of no better example of such "victimless crime" legislation more deserving of our contempt than the interstate commerce gun control regulations. While it is never "evil in itself" (*malum in se*) for a peaceable American to buy a gun across State lines (just like a bottle of beer), Congress has deemed such a "wrong prohibited" with prison and fines. As Emerson wrote:

> *Every actual State is corrupt. Good men must not obey the laws too well.*

If questioned for transacting out-of-State

First, *never* tell attendees that you're nonlocal. (At a Reno show, you're from Vegas.) If asked if you are a State resident, you might reply *"Of course!"* and say/offer/explain/amplify *nothing further.* If the agent already knows (or seems to know) who you are and in which State you reside, then you've probably been under investigation for some time and they feel confident of making stick an out-of-State transaction bust. (This is a rare thing. Usually, they merely spot one's out-of-State plates.)

What is a *"resident"*?

Remember, *"being present in a State **with the intention** of making a home in that State"* makes you a resident of that State under Title 18. Discussing with a local friend during a visit that you plan to relocate there and make a home should qualify as *"intention."* Moreover, there is *no* statutory residency for any particular length of time (as with voting, 30 days) before making legal firearm transactions.

Your response

To the agent, assert that you *are* a resident *and then clam up.* It's easy enough to later substantiate that you are a *"resident"* (*i.e.*, your friend could confirm that you just moved in with him, or were about to). Finally, it's *worth* doing so in order to avoid a *felony* conviction based on violating some cheesy interstate commerce regulation involving a *malum prohibitum*, or victimless/non-evil "crime."

Reducing your out-of-State exposure

Park any out-of-State car blocks away from the gun show (or go with a local friend). Remove all ID and papers from your person (which will deny the BATFE agent any presumptive evidence). You do *not* have to carry ID with you! If you give the fed no instant way to dispute your claim of residency, then he cannot easily concoct probable cause for instant arrest.

The out-of-State bust is *very* rare, and you'll have to draw inordinate attention to yourself to even become noticed at all, so don't get all paranoid at gun shows.

I wouldn't, however, make a habit of exhibiting at shows outside your home state(s). You certainly do not want to give the promoter any address or phone number in a State other than the one hosting the show. This is just common sense.

AVOID ENTRAPMENT!

If *anybody* tries to chat you up about illegal stuff, such as: machine gun parts and conversions, suppressors, sawed-off barrels or stocks, explosives, stolen goods, "taking action" against the government or its officials, etc.—*firmly* announce your ignorance and disinterest.

If any of the above *persist*, threaten to immediately inform the police and/or a BATFE agent. (Regardless of whether he is or isn't a plant or snitch, he will quickly scurry off.) If he persists after your warning, then follow through on your threat. If at a gun show, go to the promoter's desk and ask for a BATFE agent. (John Ross's *Unintended Consequences* has a great scene about this sort of thing, on pages 451-53.)

As long as you're within your home State(s), *and* the guns are perfectly legal, *and* you use caution with whom you deal, and you don't say anything stupid, then you can generally relax.

BUSTING THE SELLER

to *whom*

Enticing the ignorant, stupid, or greedy seller to break a federal firearms law is the most common of BATFE stings.

Do not sell to *"straw man"* purchasers

If anybody asks if he can buy your gun *for* somebody *else*, refuse, even if such is not a *"prohibited possessor."*

Do not sell to *"prohibited possessors"* (see page 16/4)

"Even though" the party is from out-of-State, underage, a felon, etc.—absolutely refuse to transact!

the *what*

The obvious are: unregistered full-auto stuff, short barreled/overall length long guns, or other miscellaneous *NFA34* stuff. First of all, you shouldn't be owning such, and secondly, you'd be a fool to try to sell it.

the *where*

If you reside in Kalifornia, then don't sell guns in Nevada. If your BATFE agent customer has reason to believe that you're from out-of-State, then *"Lucy, ju gos som splaining to do!"*

the *how*

6. DO YOU NEED A FIREARMS LICENSE? - *Under 18 U.S.C. 922 and 923, it is unlawful for a person to engage in the business of dealing firearms without a license. A person is engaged in the business of dealing in firearms if he or she devotes time, attention, and labor to dealing in firearms* **as a regular course of trade or business with the principal objective of livelihood and profit through the repetitive purchase and resale of firearms.** *A license is not required of a person who only makes occasional sales, exchanges, or purchases of firearms for the enhancement of a personal collection or for a hobby, or who sells all or part of his or her personal collection of firearms.*

— ATF Form 4473 (5300.9) Part I (4-97)

Never admit to *any* profit on *any* transaction. *Never* claim that you are supporting yourself through private gun trading. (Even though an occasional transactional profit should not constitute a *"principal objective of livelihood and profit"* the BATFE may possibly rule otherwise.) Be *very* wary of selling a gun at the same show where you bought it, especially if a profit from a *stranger* is involved (he could be a BATman). Don't *ever* divulge what you paid for a gun, or what you sold it for. Don't haunt the gun shows to the point that everybody thinks that you're a dealer. Don't buy and resell with great frequency.

A typical bust of illegal *"nonlicensed"* gun profits

To bust a seller would take two agents: one to sell an underpriced gun, and the other to buy it later at the market price (which means a profit for the victim, and thus an arrest). A possible way to avoid this is to share a table with a buddy. When one of you buys a gun, *trade* it to the other and let *him* sell it. Proving a monetary profit in that scenario would be difficult.

If you're from out-of-state, don't be stupid

As I earlier explained, the out-of-state bust is pretty rare, but showing up at the Nevada flea market with Oregon plates week after week will get somebody's attention. Registering for Georgia gun shows with a Florida address and phone is just begging for trouble. Don't . . . be . . . *stupid.*

A Boston real-life story

I had once had a gun show table with a pre-ban AR15 for sale. Two guys came up to look at it. They were immediately suspicious to me because their traffic pattern was unusual. Most gun show attendees walk the aisles from end to end, but these guys made a beeline to my table from a couple of aisles away. So, I went Condition Orange.

My AR15 had a pre-ban serial number. When I pointed this out, one guy produced a list of AR15 manufacturers and their pre-ban cutoff serial numbers. He allegedly got it off the Net. (First time I'd seen *that.* Red flag #2.)

They left to find a third buddy so the buyer could borrow some money. In 5 minutes, all three showed up. Now, I was *really* on alert for BATFE agents at gun shows usually work in teams (to corroborate their story in court). After couple of more minutes of talking, I heard (just barely) the third guy say to one of his buddies, *"We sure don't have shows like this in Georgia."*

I asked them all, *"You guys are from <u>Georgia</u>?"* When they all nodded their heads, I sharply told the prospective buyer, *"Put that down now!"* He immediately complied. I then coolly explained that private sales were not legal for out-of-state buyers, and that it would be a felony to transact.

They (poorly) feigned surprise at this, said that they were military TDY and thought that rifles were exempt. (Uh, *no* . . .)

I warned them not to try to buy firearms outside an FFL dealer, and they quickly walked off. I never saw them again.

So, beware if you hear/see anything about the buyer which seems to indicate his out-of-state status. I've had to decline several sales when some guy opened his wallet for the cash and I saw his California driver's license in the window. (It is painful lose such a sale, but a felony bust just ain't worth it!)

BUSTING THE BUYER

from *whom*
Do not buy from a *"prohibited possessor"*
If you know/have reasonable cause to believe . . . *avoid.*

the *what*
Don't buy illegal guns or full-auto parts, especially from strangers. The BATFE has ruled that owning a semi-auto rifle (say, an AR15) with even *one* full-auto part (*e.g.,* a hammer, disconnector, etc.) constitutes an illegal full-auto gun—*even if the gun cannot fire full-auto!* Heck, they've ruled that *one* full-auto part in the home of a semi-auto owner is a felony!

Inspect military SLRs for full-auto parts *before* you buy!
The chances of this for AR15s are about 5%, given public ignorance and parts interchangeability. If you're shopping for a military-pattern SLR, inspect the trigger group and bolt carrier. If the selector moves to the "auto" position, avoid!

the *where*
Don't buy outside your State(s), especially from strangers.

the *how*
Don't buy in such a way as to illegally evade the NICBC or Form 4473 requirements, or to evade them for somebody else.

Do not buy a gun *for* somebody else
A nonlicensed person cannot buy a gun *for* anybody, except to *give* as a gift. So, if any stranger or "new" friend asks you to buy a gun *for* him (this is called a *"straw man sale"*), you should politely refuse, even if the end recipient is allegedly not a *"prohibited possessor."*

BUSTING THE OWNER

Since owning something bypasses any *transactional* risk, the BATmen will either have to spot you with something, or get a tip from a snitch. Don't let strangers handle or inspect your guns (especially semi-autos). Don't talk about sensitive items, not even to friends (as their phones may be tapped).

the *who*

"Prohibited possessors" may not own guns or ammo.

the *what*

Do not own illegal full-auto guns, or even full-auto parts!

This is a stupid and unnecessary risk. Avoid! And if you do, certainly do *not* tell your wife or girlfriend:

> *Of interest, is that most cases* [in which I testify as an expert witness] *have to do with the possession of an unregistered machine gun. In almost every instance a crime of violence was not committed but rather a wife, ex-girlfriend, etc., got angry and turned their husband or boyfriend in for possession.*
> — John Norrell, *The Small Arms Review,* 11/99, p. 39

the *where*

Do not take legal guns to restricted areas!

Such may include government buildings, school property, bars, polling places on election day, etc. Know before you go.

Do not take illegal guns to gun shows or ranges!

You shouldn't be owning them in first place, but taking them out in public is just begging for trouble.

IF EVER QUESTIONED

If you are ever questioned by a law enforcement official (or by anybody who merely *seems* to ask too many personal questions), *beware*! You may be moments away from a felony arrest based on some violation (mistakenly perceived, or even maliciously concocted) of the gun regulations found in Title 18.

Ascertain his identity. Don't cower!

Once he formally announces himself a BATFE agent, politely yet firmly insist to inspect his credentials. (To "inspect" means exactly that—not letting him merely "flash" his "fold.") He will usually do this, albeit reluctantly. Since you've probably never seen a federal badge before, you might then (if you feel like pushing things a bit) firmly ask for corroborating ID such as his driver's license (which might have his home address on it). *This* he will rarely show you! How you play it from there is your choice; you could accept his badge, *or* you could maintain his badge to be phony and that he's *not* a federal agent (which will *really* piss him off). Either way, you've made your point.

What's the *relationship*? Arrest? Detention?

Immediately ascertain if it's an arrest, detention, or contact. Then you'll understand his powers versus your rights.

First, ask if you are under arrest

He'll ask for your full name, ID, an address, how long you've lived there, etc. *Do not answer!* Instead, "answer" a question with a question. **Ask if you are under *arrest*.** (What you are doing is acting like a Free American who demands to know why his Liberty is being interrupted.)

If not under arrest, then ask if you are being detained

He's more likely merely *"contact"* fishing, during which you may cheerfully bid him *"Good day!"* and walk away. If he replies that you *are* being detained, ask him to articulate his reasonable suspicion. This will give him great pause, as most Americans, law-abiding or not, do not know to demand this. He might then ask if you are an attorney. Coolly reply, *"That is not relevant to the issue at hand. What is your reasonable suspicion?"* Only attorneys speak this way, and his confidence will *really* begin to ebb at this point, trust me!

Reasonable suspicion is the "little brother" of probable cause, and gives the officer the authority to detain you (20-30 minutes will be considered acceptable by any court). During this time you may not leave, and he is permitted to physically restrain you if necessary. He is trying to build reasonable suspicion into arrestable probable cause, and will bombard you with many questions in an intimidating manner. (During a detention, he is not required to "Mirandize" you; that's only *after* arrest.) **Know this: You cannot *ever* be forced to give testimony about *yourself*!** You do *not* have to answer questions during a contact, or a detention (except your name), or during an arrest. Reply that *if* he has valid probable cause to arrest, then he's welcome to do so, but you've got *nothing* to say without your lawyer present. *Period. End of story.*

If detained, repeatedly ask if you're free to go

At first he will likely say *"No"* and follow with yet another question. (He might then pat you down for concealed weapons, but he cannot actually search your pockets, wallet, or sealed/locked containers.) You should reply, *"I have nothing to say without my lawyer present. Am I free to go?"* That's your mantra. Don't deviate from it. "Run out the clock" and he will eventually *have* to release you. He can't detain you forever.

Once free to go, don't hang around

As soon as he says that you're free to go, the relationship has changed from detention to mere contact (from which you may leave). First, call your lawyer and explain what happened. Then, exit the premises immediately. If the scene was eerie enough (or if they're following you to the parking lot), then take a taxi and have a friend pick up your car later.

While all this may sound extreme, **nobody *else* can equally protect your own rights and liberty.** *Any* personal questioning by police is an adversarial relationship, and you must utterly be on guard. Please read my *You & The Police!* to fully understand your rights during any police confrontation. To quote myself, *"Cops work for the State, and the State is in search of bodies."* Don't be a "customer" of the State!

IF ARRESTED, EXPLAIN *NOTHING!*

You have only two duties during a search or arrest: to shut up and to stay alert. If ever arrested, *offer or explain nothing*! They went to a *lot* of trouble to get a signed warrant, and they're not going to be talked out of their hard work by even the most plausible of excuses. There is *nothing* you can say at the Scene to make them undo what they've just done. It's *their* party. You're already in a hole, and each word you say is shovelful of dirt to dig yourself even deeper. The only thing to say is *"I do not consent to any search of my premises or property. I do not desire to answer any questions. I want to call my lawyer immediately."*

Don't give them *any* clues to your possible defense

If you do, they will undermine it (and they are very good at that). They surprised *you*, so your lawyer should surprise *them* later in court. *Nobody* can think of everything—not the criminals, and even not the *cops*. Believe me, they'll have goofed on *something,* and with diligence you'll discover it.

Do not be tempted by an urge to mentally spar with them

They do this for a living—you *don't*. The most brilliant display of intellectual swordsmanship I ever saw was in *The Man For All Seasons* (Sir Thomas More played by Paul Scofield). What succulent dueling with Master Secretary Cromwell and the court! Did he win? *No.* While he won all his battles, he lost the war by needlessly debating with a King's agent (who later perjured himself). Moral: If Sir Thomas More can be hung by his own tongue, then surely *you* can be, too!

"Never interrupt an enemy while he is making a mistake"

Wise advice from Napoleon. If they are breaking the law, or even proper procedure, allow them to continue. It'll somehow backfire on them later to either destroy their assertion of *"good faith"* or to weaken/negate material evidence.

Control your attitude! Stay calm and alert!

Be calm (keep the Scene to a minimum), polite (it can never hurt, and it often helps), and *alert.*

Observe and listen to *everything* going on. (Since you're not running your mouth, this ought to be easy.) They are as excited as you are (though obviously from a different perspective), and they too will make mistakes. Demand to know who is in charge, and to see his badge. Demand to see the warrant. Listen for other names (they won't always be wearing name tags or badges). Try to glean a sense of what they *know* versus what they only *suspect*.

Beware of tricks!

If they ask you to handle an item, *refuse*! (Why put your prints on something that did not necessarily have them before?) Don't admit to any technical or legal expertise, which could be later used against you. If they claim that so-and-so has already implicated you in some alleged crime, shrug your shoulders and blandly reply, *"See you in court, then."* If they claim to *"know all about it,"* calmly reply, *"Good, then you can explain it all to me."*

Admittedly, these lines verge on the smartass, so if you don't feel comfortable with using them, fine. Just keep refusing to answer any questions before speaking to your lawyer.

Ownership vs. *"possessory interest"*

If they ask if a particular thing belongs to you, *beware*! Refuse to answer, but if for some reason you felt *truly* compelled to claim it, admit to merely a *"possessory interest."* (This is, for example, what a coatcheck girl should say if drugs were found in a patron's garment.) *"Possessory interest"* means that you have temporary control or responsibility over something that isn't yours (or isn't yours yet). Point being, the phrase justifies an item being in your possession, but leaves an "out" regarding ownership and full knowledge of its nature or contents. (Or, as our Government loves to say, *"plausible deniability."*) It also allows you to exercise 4th Amendment rights on behalf another's property, as you have temporary custody for it, remember? Still, I wouldn't admit to even *"possessory interest"* of an item unless you *absolutely* knew what you're doing.

Protecting yourself in advance with photos/witnesses

Regarding any military-pattern SLR, it's a good idea to precisely document its legal status. Then, you can later prove any tampering of it by the authorities.

Make a detailed description of the gun. Have only one file per gun (and don't give the files obvious gun names!), encrypt it with PGP's biggest key, and store the file(s) only on a ZIP disk (never on the hard drive). Store the disk offsite.

Next, take quality photos (make triple prints) of its semi-auto trigger group and receiver. Use *film*, not digital photos (which can be alleged to have been computer-altered).

Staple each photo set to a printed description of the gun, and have two or more witnesses date and sign the lot. Give one copy to your lawyer, and the others to your witnesses. *"Why not keep a copy for yourself?"* Because during a search or raid, it would likely be found and thus tip off the feds to your protection (which they might then illegally circumvent to keep their case).

Imagine the Government's surprise when their bogus case (based on an altered gun) falls apart in court with the testimony of two witnesses and photo evidence! (At the minimum, such evidence would clearly establish *"reasonable doubt."*) In any victory, preparation is everything.

Proving criminal intent (*mens rea*)

Actus non facit reum, nisi mens est rea.
The act does not make a man guilty, unless the mind be guilty.

Remember, the law usually requires you *"know or have reasonable cause to believe"* that your actions were illegal. This element (one of several) is under the *Government's* burden of proof. An otherwise viable prosecution can easily stumble and fail on the *mens rea* burden, even if the other elements are indisputable. Unless the defendant has admitted (in a diary, over the phone, to a witness, etc.) that he *knew* his actions were illegal, such is very difficult to prove. (Watch your tongue!)

On this note, it's probably a good idea to purge your home of any evidence that you understood the regulations, such as law books, news articles, letters, and even this book.

Know a good gun-rights lawyer

The JPFO or GOA can help you find one. I'd look for one now, *before* you ever possibly need him. If you believe that you *are* under investigation or the potential victim of a sting, then get the relationship going immediately (while you store offsite any "extra" guns). Make sure that your family and friends know how to contact him, in case you can't.

Final comments

*When after having thus successively taken each member of the community in its powerful grasp, and fashioned him at will, the supreme power then extends its arm over the whole community. **It covers the surface of society with a network of small complicated rules,** minute and uniform, through which the most original minds and the most energetic characters cannot penetrate to rise above the crowd. **The will of man is not shattered but softened, bent and guided; men are seldom forced by it to act,***

but they are constantly retrained from acting. *Such a power does not destroy, but it prevents existence; it does not tyrannize, but it compresses, enervates, extinguishes, and stupefies a people, **till each nation is reduced to be nothing better that a flock of timid and industrial animals, of which government is the shepherd.** I have always thought that servitude of the regular, quiet, and gentle kind which I have just described **might be combined more easily than is commonly believed with some of the outward forms of freedom** and that it might even establish itself under the wing of the sovereignty of the people.*
— Alexis de Tocqueville, *Democracy in America* (1835)

There is a clear line crossed by the Government when we should no longer be *"bent and guided"* by that *"network of small complicated* rules." And that is ...

The Day of Confiscation. When they come for your *"assault rifles"* you've got only one *last* chance to use them.

It seems very possible, if not likely, that military-style rifles will first be coercively registered, then banned, and then confiscated. Really, the only question to ask yourself right now is if you will fight with your battle rifles, or without them?

Does the date of 19 April 1775 mean anything to you?

Now and later, I urge you to always keep things in proper perspective. Yes, *"Discretion is the better part of valor"*—**until there is no *choice* but to be brave.** If and when that time ever comes, we will surely know it.

May God grant us the wisdom to discover the right, the will to choose it, and the strength to make it endure.
— King Arthur, from the movie *First Knight*

WHAT ABOUT OUR RECENT SUPREME COURT "VICTORIES?"

Technically, we're 4 for 4 since 1992:

Thompson Center in 1992 (BATF rules on short-barreled rifles)

Staples in 1994 (knowledge required to prove illegal possession of an automatic weapon)

Lopez in 1995 (overturning the *"Gun-Free School Zone Act of 1991"*)

Printz in 1997 (overturning the background checks by CLEOs)

Boston sez: Hold off on the party balloons

> *The federal judiciary these days is not a competing power, anxious to keep the executive and legislative branches hemmed inside Constitutional bounds. It is a co-conspirator, sternly holding the people down while allowing our voracious oppressors to commit unbridled mayhem any way they please.*
> — Vin Suprynowicz, *Send in the Waco Killers* (1999), p. 465

I had observed the same thing two years earlier in *Hologram of Liberty*, so I am heartened that others are also realizing it too.

Point #1: A new broom sweeps clean. Four victories in a decade does *not* constitute a solid, irreversible trend.

Point #2: They were all 5-4 decisions. Expect Rehnquist or O'Connor to flip soon. The Scalia/Thomas "glue" won't hold.

Point #3: Two of those cases involved *federalism* challenges, *not* 2nd Amendment challenges. The Court *could* have by now struck down *NFA34* and *GCA68*, but has so far denied *cert* to the potential landmark gun cases.

Point #4: The Court is unwilling to go "too far" in restoring our 2nd Amendment rights. For example, it *could* have killed Brady's 5-day waiting period by now, but has not. Nobody, not even Scalia, has ever joined Thomas's concurrences.

Point #5: Even if these victories *are* a trend, and even if the 5-4 majority *does* hold firm, and even if the Court *were* serious about upholding our rights, there's still the presidential power of executive order (based on some nebulous *"national emergency"* such as 9/11 Part 2). Show me just *one* executive order overturned by the Supreme Court in the last 60 years!

I trust I make my melancholy case. Even if I'm wrong, it's still no huge problem for the more pesky Justices to be the victim of a fatal mugging (this nearly happened to Justice Souter while he was jogging), have a fatal one-car accident, or, best yet, shoot themselves in an unprecedented, baffling moment of suicidal despair. (Ask Vince Foster how this works.)

After 9/11, commercial pilots are pleading for their right to protect their planes and passengers, **but *evil* Congressmen are still trying to block a pilot's right to be armed.** Yes, I said *"evil"* because not even Congressmen can be so stupid. Look Charles Schumer, we tried your *"gun free zone"* and it got

3,000 people killed in 90 minutes! There is not *one* compelling reason for keeping our airline pilots disarmed (we trust them with our lives anyway!), and armed pilots would eliminate the silly and expensive plan for 20,000 new sky marshals.

Americans should be in an *uproar* that our pilots are forbidden to be armed. They're not. **The pilots' unions should be *on strike* over this.** They're not. The USA is full of cowards, and I am profoundly ashamed about this.

The victim disarmament clan have a timetable to keep, they're on a roll, and, most importantly, they're not afraid of us. With or without the Court's blessing, the feds are going to try to strip away more and more of our self-defense rights.

They won't stop until—*unless*—they become afraid of us. History has proven that in countless examples. In *The Gulag Archipelago*, Alexander Solzhenitsyn persuasively argued that had Stalin's goons been assaulted at least with wooden chairs and kitchen knives during the initial raids, the police state would have collapsed from a lack of thugs willing to volunteer for such hazardous duty. Thugs became thugs in the first place because they're *jackals* at heart. They shoot nursing mothers in the face from 200yds and pour helicopter machine gun fire on helpless families in homestead churches. *Cowards*.

We'll have *no excuse*. We have the best firearms in history, we are the most armed people on the planet, we have an ingrained tradition of Liberty, and we have the priceless benefit of historical hindsight to understand not just the *process* of gradual tyranny, but its ugly finale of demonization, ostracization, roundups, camps (ask the Japanese-Americans of WWII), "reeducation," confinement, torture, and executions.

We will have *no excuse* not to resist.

OUR DWINDLING RIGHTS

OUR BILL OF RIGHTS

The following material comes from my *Hologram of Liberty* (1997), pages 4/1-8. It is highly relevant to understanding the Bill of Rights (tacked on by a very reluctant Federalist Congress), and how/why little of it remains today.

Congress (predictably) stalls on Bill of Rights

The Philadelphia Convention [putatively] *omitted a Bill of Rights only because its members thought that very limited powers were* [expressly] *granted to the new federal government. They supposed that confining Congress to the exercise of the delegated powers would itself eliminate any threat to fundamental rights, and that inclusion of a Bill of Rights would...suggest a loose construction of the delegated powers, which would be an even greater threat to liberty.*

The people were not satisfied by this rather technical, lawyers' argument. (And rightfully not. BTP)
— Archibald Cox; *The Court and the Constitution*, p. 38

A number of states had accepted the [Constitution] *with urgent recommendations for changes. At first it seemed that Congress would pay no attention to these suggestions.* **Patrick Henry and others then set up a clamor which had to be heeded,** *and Congress referred the proposals* [from various states] *to a committee.* **...the Congressional majority threw out all suggestions for altering the scheme of government...**
— Nevins and Commager; *Pocket History of the U.S.*, p. 132

Public restlessness at the lack of a bill of rights became acute. New Yorkers made an issue of federalist John Jay's circular letter to Governor Clinton, which promised a second convention to adopt amendments. Alarmed at this prospect, Madison privately listed four grounds for passing a Bill of Rights: "❶ *to prove* [federalists] *friends of liberty,* ❷ *remove remaining inquietudes,* ❸ *bring in N.C. and R.I.,* ❹ *to improve the Constitution.*" (Notice his priorities.)

Derailing the second-convention movement, Madison moved that the House begin, on 25 May 1789, considering the promised bill of rights. House federalists, however, argued that adopting new tax laws and organizing the government were more important. (Figures.) Madison then enlisted the help of President Washington, who wrote on 31 May that amendments *"are necessary to quiet the fears of some respectable characters and well-meaning men."* (Having achieved their national government, Washington *et al* could afford to be magnanimous and ceased their petty insults of the *Antis.*) On 8 June, Madison spoke to the House:

> And I do most sincerely believe that if congress will devote but one day to this subject, so far as to satisfy the public that we do not disregard their wishes, it will have a salutary influence on the public councils, **and prepare the way for a favorable reception of our future measures.**

Meaning, *"Just because we're on-line doesn't mean that we're home free. We've got to shut up this racket, or else the states will force a second convention—and who knows what could happen then!"* The House finally "saw the light." Convening a 13 member committee (5 of whom were Convention delegates), they hurriedly drafted seventeen proposals culled from Madison's study of the over *200* submitted by the states.

The federalist Senate (with only two *Antis* out of 22 members), however, was less cheerful about a bill of rights than even the House. Meeting behind closed doors without record of their debates, the Senate reduced the number of proposed amendments from 17 to 12 and largely gutted what little strength the House gave them. A "conference committee" of 3 Reps and 3 Senators restored many of them, and their version was passed by Congress in late September. The states ratified 10 of the 12 by 15 December 1791.

Madison, who would later soften some of his sharper federalist edges, deserves credit for pushing the amendments through a clearly reluctant House. Without his persistence, we likely would *never* have had a Bill of Rights.

Our purposely diluted Bill of Rights

Let us understand that these 10 amendments were a scrappy bone, *very* grudgingly thrown to the people.

> [Madison] *ignored all the recommendations that addressed the powers of government:* nothing on taxation as a last resort (a provision that appeared on every list), nothing on two-thirds votes [from both houses] for treaties, trade laws, or standing armies in peacetime, nothing toward the prohibition of monopolies (urged by every state except Virginia). *There was nothing that looked like the grand charter of rights Mason and Henry had envisioned as a preface to the Constitution;...*
> — Henry Mayer; *A Son of Thunder,* p. 455

Not only that, but the amendments which *were* offered had been written in alarmingly equivocal language which the courts have used over generations to whittle away our rights:

The **1st** Amendment forbids only *"prohibiting"* the free exercise of religion—not infringement. (Ask the polygamist Mormons.) It also seems to invite the interpretation of protected speech being that solely of *political* content.

The **2nd** Amendment protecting the right to keep and bear arms was couched within a seemingly subordinate clause (begging for recent confusion), placing such under the auspice of an organized state militia (which did not even exist in 1789).

The **3rd** allows the quartering of soldiers in private houses without the owners' consent *if prescribed by law.* During some future martial law, we may indeed see this occur. (Why do you think the modern Census questionnaires demand such detailed information about your dwelling?)

Searches and seizures are permitted in the **4th** if they are not *"unreasonable"* (whatever that is), and the courts have carved out at least *14* exceptions to the warrant requirement.

"Due process of law" is now a sick joke. In the **5th**, only *"capital"* or *"infamous"* crimes require grand jury indictments

and this is bypassed in the military or during *"time of war or public danger"* (whatever that is).

The protection against double jeopardy is gone, for you may be retried for a state offense in federal court as a *"civil rights violation."*

According to the 2004 **Hiibel** ruling, you cannot withhold your name if asked during a detention.

The Government may take private property for public use as long as the owner has been paid *"just compensation"* (calculated by the feds, of course). In the 1928 **Springer** case (277 US 189, 210), Chief Justice Holmes dissented:

> *Property must not be taken without compensation* (He conveniently omitted *"just"* from *"just compensation."* BTP)*, but with the help of a phrase (the police power) some property may be taken or destroyed for public use without paying for it, if you do not take too much.*

In the **6th**, the Court has ruled (in **Blanton**) that *"all criminal prosecutions"* means only *"capital"* crimes as described in the 5th. (*Wink, wink.* This is *Animal Farm*-style "except-for" jurisprudence.) You've no right to a jury trial for crimes with sentences less than six months, even if charged with multiple misdemeanors with a total punishment exceeding such.

Also, a *"speedy trial"* should have been defined, and the right to non-licensed *"counsel"* should have been clearly guaranteed to prevent the establishment of a legal nobility.

In the **7th**, *"according to the rules of common law"* allows federal courts reversible review of jury verdicts.

In the **8th**, the definitions of *"excessive"* bail and fines and *"cruel and unusual punishment"* were purposely left to the whimsical interpretation of federal courts. Today, during the (Forever) War On Terrorism, the issue of torture is seriously being debated by legal scholars as a necessary expedient.

The **9th** Amendment was well put, though robbed of its practical value by the Constitution as a whole.

The **10th** Amendment was, in a vivid portent of things to come, emasculated by Madison's refusal to strictly limit the Federal Government's broad *"delegated"* powers—even though *"expressly delegated"* was promised to the states in John Jay's circular letter. The feds can do any I:8:17 *"necessary"* thing they were merely *"delegated"* to do.

"Necessary" (allowing implied/implicit/consequential powers) is not the same as *"absolutely necessary"* (as was applied to the States in I:10:2). We lost our country because of the omission of just two words: *"absolutely"* and *"expressly."*

We were thrown a sop and told, *"There are your precious amendments—now shut up!"* Today, we have no *real* freedom of religion or of the press, no *real* right to keep and bear arms, no *real* right to a jury trial or counsel of one's choice, and no *meaningful* limit to federal expansion. We've only *permissions.*

The Constitution is actually an open-ended document and the Bill of Rights merely contains ten speed bumps in the road to Tyranny. Not that I'm wholly ungrateful. Speed bumps are better than nothing, I guess:

> **Imagine where we would be today if...the lack of a Bill of Rights had not been taken up as the major concern of the anti-federalists, such as Patrick Henry.** We would be trusting our rights and liberties to the reading of the Attorney General, who today (this was in 1987) believes that people who are defendants in criminal trials are probably guilty or they would not be defendants,...
> — E.L. Doctorow; from *The Nation*

JUDICIAL TYRANNY

I wish that our effective rights, whittled away as they are, could yet remain *in stasis.* Such is pipe dream. The onslaught continues, especially due to 9/11. This book may very well end up a small, bitter slice of legal nostalgia by 2015, if not sooner.

> The Constitution just sets minimums... Most of the rights that you enjoy go way beyond what the Constitution requires [under Supreme Court interpretation].
> — Justice Antonin Scalia, in a March 2003 speech at John Carroll University in Ohio

The federal courts, especially the Supreme Court, have actively removed many Constitutional safeguards, the most notable being your right to a trial by jury in all criminal trials. In a horrific bit of *Animal Farm* "except for" jurisprudence (***Blanton v. North Las Vegas***, 489 US 541), the Supreme Court ruled that offenses carrying less than six months imprisonment are deemed *"petty offenses"* in which the 6th

Amendment right to jury trials is *inapplicable.* Funny, I don't recall the 6th Amendment mentioning *"petty offenses:"*

In ALL criminal prosecutions, the accused shall enjoy the right to a speedy and public trial, by an impartial jury... (my emphasis)

When *"all"* can mean "some," the handwriting is on the wall.

Blanton doctrine was upheld in early 1993 when a drunk driver in Yosemite National Park was denied a jury trial and sued the Government. The Court ruled 9-0 (***U.S. v. Nachtigal***, 113 S.Ct. 1072) that there is *no* constitutional right to a jury trial for drunk driving committed on federal territory (a *"petty offense"*). This was no disputable point of law—the Court ruled *unanimously.* ("Land of the free," indeed!)

Because of 9/11, it's a Brave New World. All bets are off. Consider the 2004 case of **Hiibel** which ruled that you no longer have the absolute right to remain silent during a detention.

Or the so-called *Bipartisan Campaign Reform Act* of 2002 (BCRA) upheld 5-4 by the Court in ***McConnell v. FEC*** (2003) which requires *"electioneering communications"* just before federal elections to be financed solely through "hard" money contributions (*i.e.*, from individuals and PACs) subject to contribution limits and disclosure requirements.

CONGRESSIONAL TYRANNY

Much of the Federal Government's expansion has been accomplished through Congressional application of their Constitutional treaty power (VI:2) and the interstate commerce clause (I:8:3). These two "wild card" powers allow Congress to circumvent any and all Constitutional restrictions. (This is fully covered in my *Hologram of Liberty.*)

Congress has gotten so bold that it doesn't even resort to its "wild cards" anymore. Case in point: H.R. 666.

House Resolution 666

The *"exclusionary rule"* (***Mapp v. Ohio*** of 1961) is loathed by the government, and was attacked by H.R. 666 (not enumerated in the AP wire story, for obvious reasons!), the so-called

Exclusionary Rule Reform Act of 1995. Such would have, in *federal* cases, abolished the historical requirement of a warrant prior to entry of your house. Kick down doors, warrantless searches/arrests (and their resulting evidence, normally the *"fruit of the poisoned tree"*) would have been upheld if the feds claimed such were in *"good faith"* compliance with the 4th Amendment. Since Congress cannot unilaterally get rid of the 4th, Congress proposed to allow the federal stormtroopers to merely pay "lip service" to it!

The state of political/legal ignorance is such that this ludicrous proposition was pretty much swallowed whole. When the legislature may, at its pleasure, so basely abrogate its operating charter because of a bovine, feeding-at-the-public-trough constituency, liberty is clearly on its deathbed.

We *can* halt this, however. You need to spread the word about a concept once discussed in civics classes: **Congress *cannot*, on its own, render void the Constitution.** For if it can, as the 1933 German parliament bypassed the Weimar Constitution after the Nazi-staged Reichstag fire, then we are on a short road to fascism. (Read *The Ominous Parallels* by Leonard Peikoff.)

EXECUTIVE ORDERS / MARTIAL LAW

[This new proposed Bureau of Investigation could become a] *system of spying upon and espionage of the people, such as has prevailed in Russia.*
　　— a worried U.S. Congress in 1908

When the gradual methods don't work, the State becomes desperate and sloughs off all façades of legality. This is called martial law. The people become, finally, utter subjects to the executive authority. This *can* happen *here*.

If it *does*, then this little book will serve only as a bitter reminder to the marginal freedom we once enjoyed. You can tell your children, *"In my day, back in '05, we'd demand the police to state their 'reasonable suspicion' and they'd back off!"*

The supposition of this book is—that with adequate numbers of courageous folks, newly trained in the basics of Constitutional law—we can grind to a halt further encroachments of our Liberty. When a great weight is pressing upon you, it must first be stopped before it can be cast off. *You & The Police!* is about stopping the weight. Casting it off is another story for other books, such as *Good-Bye April 15th!* and *Molôn Labé!*

This weight of tyranny, even *slightly* further pressed against us, will materialize as martial law. I'm talking biometric IDs, curfews, currency exchange restrictions, equity transfer moratoriums, a new incontrovertible "dollar," mandatory civil service, roadblock checkpoints, etc. When the President says, *"Jump!"* you'll reply, *"Yes, Sir!—how high?"*

It *can* happen here. If Hitler happened in the land of Bach and Goethe, tyranny can happen in the land of Jefferson.

This martial law will be based on the 1917 *Trading With The Enemy Act* and similar wartime acts of WWII and Korea. We've been in a state of "national emergency" since at least 1933, and maybe even since 1917. **More shocking still, the roots for this lie in the *Constitution*,** which allows (in I:9:2) the suspension of at least the *"privilege of the writ of habeas corpus...when in cases...the public safety may require it."* Our state of "national emergency" has never been rescinded, to my knowledge. (Read Dr. Eugene Schroder's *The Constitution: Fact Or Fiction.* ISBN 1-885534-06-X)

USA PATRIOT Act of 2001

This coarse Orwellianism stands for *"Uniting and Strengthening America by Providing Appropriate Tools Required to Intercept and Obstruct Terrorism."* (The acronymania is getting pretty ridiculous.)

*Moreover, as America becomes an increasingly multicultural society, it may find it more difficult to fashion a consensus on foreign policy issues, **except in the circumstance of a truly massive and widely perceived direct external threat.***
— Zbigniew Brezezinki, "The Grand Chessboard" (1997)

Perhaps the universe is nothing but an equilibrium of idiocies.
— George Santayana

Watch what you read in public . . .

. . . or some "good citizen" will call the FBI on you. A free-lance writer in Atlanta had two agents come to interview him:

> I'll tell you what, Marc. Someone in the (coffee) shop that day saw you reading something and thought it looked suspicious enough to call us about. So that's why we're here, just checking it out. Like I said, there's no problem. We'd just like to get to the bottom of this. Now if we can't then you may have a problem. And you don't want that.

What was the "suspicious" article? Something called "Weapons of Mass Stupidity." And whoever was snoopy enough to catch the title actually followed the reader out to the parking lot to write down his plate number. When challenged about the waste of Bureau time, FBI Atlanta spokesman Joe Parris said, *"In this post-911 era, it is the absolute responsibility of the FBI to follow up on any tips of potential terrorist activity. Are people going to take exception and be inconvenienced by this at times? Oh, yeah. ...A certain amount of convenience is going to be offset by an increase in security."* For the full story, click on:

http://atalanta.creativeloafing.com/2003-07-17/rant.html

> The drug warriors and anti-gun zealots love the new powers that now can be used to watch the every move of our citizens. "Extremists" who talk of the Constitution, promote right-to-life, form citizen militias, or participate in nonmainstream religious practices now can be monitored much more effectively by those who find their views offensive. Laws recently passed by Congress apply to all Americans, not just terrorists. But we should remember that if the terrorists are known and identified, existing law would have been quite adequate to deal with them.
>
> — Congressman Ron Paul, www.jpgo.org/paul-target.html

The *USA PATRIOT Act* would *not* have prevented 9/11

> A full eight months after September 11, the Bush administration was forced to backtrack from its earlier denials and admit that the FBI and CIA had received several warnings that Al Qaeda network members were taking flight lessons and had plans to hijack commercial airplanes in the United States. The government has admitted that its failure to heed the warning was not because of a lack of law enforcement powers. Rather, the failure was the result of an information overload, a lack trained translators, and communication failures within and between intelligence agencies.
>
> — Nancy Chang, *Silencing Political Dissent* (2002), p.16

AMERICA'S FUTURE

The man who lives under the servitude of laws, takes, without suspecting it, the soul of a slave.
— George Ripert, *Le Déclin du Droit*

Oh, it "can't happen in *America?*" The assertion contains its own rebuttal: it *will* happen here precisely because nobody believes it possible. History seems to love ironies, and the greatest irony imaginable is that *the most free nation ever in human record* could become totalitarian. America has a deep, nosy, puritanical streak which is just the kind of fertile "spy-on-your-neighbor" soil necessary to an empowered State. There are millions of pious left-lane loiterers who literally *delight* in slowing down highway traffic to the silly speed limit.

> *The battle for personal liberty seems to have been attained,* **but in the absence of the din and clash, we cannot comprehend the meaning of the safeguards employed...** *The oppression of the crowns and principalities is unquestionably over,* **and merciless majorities may yet constitute one of the chapters of future history** [of new and vicious oppression].
> — *U.S. v. James,* 60 F. 264, 265 (1894)

"Can't happen here"—*Ha!* I can't envision it happening anywhere *else*. Practically every other nation has gone through this, and given our patent lack of "vaccinations" we're long overdue for some *real* tyranny. The *USA PATRIOT Act* is the foundation for a very tall edifice.

It is *so* close to happening here because the entire country is dead asleep in a drunken stupor of materialism, apathy, and gutlessness. Congress proposed to abolish the 4th Amendment, even titling the thing in demonic fashion as H.R. 666, and everybody remained inexorably glued to the O.J. trial.

I'm not enthusiastic about the *immediate* prognosis for Liberty. I'm only a hopeless optimist in the long run. Truth and righteousness are marathoners, while lies and evil merely sprint. The sprinters always lose their wind. This is a race between the Tortoise and the Hare. **We are witnessing the *last* sprint of the Hare.** He will plot and cheat and will seemingly have the Tortoise beat, but he will lose.

The "fat lady" of freedom has yet to sing.

Works by Boston T. Party:

Good-Bye April 15th!
The untaxation classic—crystal clear and sweeping. Copied, plagiarized, and borrowed from, but never equaled. The most effective and least hazardous untaxation guide. Proven over 12 years and thousands of readers!

    392 pp. softcover (1992) $40 + $6 s&h (cash, please)

You & The Police!   (revised for 2005)
The definitive guide to your rights and tactics during police confrontations. When can you *refuse* to answer questions or consent to searches? Don't lose your liberty through ignorance! This 2005 edition covers the *USA PATRIOT Act* and much more.

    168 pp. softcover (2005) $16 + $5 s&h (cash, please)

Bulletproof Privacy
How to Live Hidden, Happy, and Free!
Explains precisely how to lay low and be left alone by the snoops, government agents and bureaucrats. Boston shares many of his own unique methods. The bestselling privacy book in America!

    160 pp. softcover (1997) $16 + $5 s&h (cash, please)

Hologram of Liberty
The Constitution's Shocking Alliance
with Big Government   by Kenneth W. Royce
The Convention of 1787 was the most brilliant and subtle *coup d'état* in history. The nationalist framers *designed* a strong government, guaranteed through purposely ambiguous verbiage. Many readers say this is Boston's best book. A jaw-dropper.

    262 pp. softcover (1997) $20 + $5 s&h (cash, please)

Boston on Surviving Y2K
And Other Lovely Disasters
Even though Y2K was Y2¿*Qué?* this title remains highly useful for all preparedness planning. **Now on sale for 50% off!** (It's the same book as The Military Book Club's *Surviving Doomsday*.)

    352 pp. softcover (1998) only $11 + $5 s&h (in cash)

Boston's Gun Bible (new text for 2004)
A rousing how-to/*why*-to on modern gun ownership. Firearms are *"liberty's teeth"* and it's time we remembered it. Fully revised in 2002 with 10 new chapters. ***200+ new pages* were added!** Much more complete than the 2000 edition. No other general gun book is more thorough or useful! Indispensable!

    848 pp. softcover (2002) $28 + $6 s&h (cash, please)

Molôn Labé!   (Boston's first novel)
If you liked *Unintended Consequences* by John Ross and Ayn Rand's *Atlas Shrugged*, then Boston's novel will be a favorite. It dramatically outlines an innovative recipe for Liberty which could actually work! A thinking book for people of action; an action book for people of thought. A freedom classic!

    454 pp. softcover (2004) $24 + $6 s&h (cash, please)
    limited edition hardcover $44 + $6 (while supplies last)

www.javelinpress.com
www.freestatewyoming.org

www.javelinpress.com

NOTE: Javelin Press is enjoying rapid growth, which may affect our address or pricing. Please verify both on our website *before* you send your order!

Prices each copy:	**Retail**	**<40%>**	**<44%>**	**<50%>**
Good-Bye April 15th! 8½"x11" 392 pp. 11/1992	1-2 copies **$40**	3-7 **$24**	8-15 **$22**	*case of 16 or more* **$20**
You & The Police! 5½"x8½" 168 pp. 2/2005	1-5 copies **$16**	(Newly revised! Visit our website for quanity discounts.)		
Bulletproof Privacy 5½"x8½" 160 pp. 1/1997	1-5 copies **$16**	6-39 **$10**	40-79 **$8.80**	*case of 80 or more* **$8**
Hologram of Liberty 5½"x8½" 262 pp. 8/1997	1-5 copies **$20**	6-19 **$12**	20-39 **$11**	*case of 40 or more* **$10**
Boston on Surviving Y2K 5½"x8½" 352 pp. 11/1998	1-5 copies **$11**	6-17 **$10**	18-35 **$9**	*case of 36 or more* **$8**
Boston's Gun Bible 5½"x8½" 848 pp. 4/2002	1-2 copies **$28**	3-7 **$16.80**	8-15 **$15.70**	*case of 16 or more* **$14**
Molôn Labé! 5½"x8½" 454 pp. 1/2004	1-5 copies **$24**	6-13 **$14.40**	14-27 **$13.44**	*case of 28 or more* **$12**

Mix titles for *any* quantity discount. This is easiest done as ¼ case per title:
¼ case of:　**GBA15!** 4　**Y&P!** 19　**BP** 20　**HoL** 10　**BoSY** 9　**BGB** 4　**ML!** 7

Shipping and Handling are *not* included!　Add below:

non-case S&H for *Good-Bye April 15th!*　*Boston's Gun Bible*　*Molôn* :
First Class (or UPS for larger orders) add: $6 for first copy, $2 each additional copy.

non-case S&H within USA for other titles (*i.e., Y&P!, BP, HoL,* **and** *BoSY***):**
First Class (or UPS for larger orders) add: $5 for first copy, $1 each additional copy.

CASE orders (straight or mixed) UPS Ground: $25 west of the Miss.; $35 east.

Overpayment will be refunded in cash with order. Underpayment will delay order! If you have questions on discounts or S&H, email us through our website.

These forms of payment *only:*

Cash (Preferred. Cash orders receive signed copies when available.)
payee blank M.O.s (Which makes them more easily negotiable.)
credit cards (Many of our distributors take them. See our website.)

Unless prior agreement has been made, *we do not accept and will return* checks, C.O.D.s, filled-in M.O.s, or any other form of tender. Prices and terms are subject to change without notice (check our website first). Please send paid orders to:

JAVELIN PRESS ● c/o P.O. Box 31Y ● Ignacio, Colorado. (81137-0031)